NONE TOO FRAGILE

Pearl Jam and Eddie Vedder

Martin Clarke

Plexus, London

This book is dedicated to Simon Dunn, for his continuing enthusiasm and support.

All rights reserved including the right of reproduction in whole or in part in any form
Copyright © 1998 by Martin Clarke
Copyright © 2015, 2009, 2008, 2005, 2003 by Plexus Publishing Ltd
Published by Plexus Publishing Limited
The Studio, Hillgate Place
18-20 Balham Hill
London SW12 9ER
www.plexusbooks.com

British Library Cataloguing in Publication Data
A catalogue record for this book is available from the British Library

ISBN-13: 978 0 85965 539 2

Designed by Phil Gambrill
Printed in Great Britain by Bell & Bain Ltd.

Acknowledgements

The following publications were extremely helpful in the writing of this book: *Rolling Stone* have covered the band's career frequently and in great depth. Other publications which proved invaluable include *The Los Angeles Times, Spin, NME, Melody Maker, Q, Vox, Select, Mojo, San Diego Reader,* the *Rocket, Rip Magazine, Musician Magazine, Seattle Weekly, BIGO* (Singapore), *Guitar School, Chicago Tribune, Denver Post, Kerrang!, Grand Royal Fanzine, Addicted To Noise, Dissident Fanzine, Guitar Player, Billboard, Bass Player Magazine, Guitar World, Washington Post, Downtown Edition, Cleveland Plain Dealer, Mr Showbiz, Modern Drummer, Scene Magazine.*

The following radio stations have also provided excellent interviews with the band: KISW 99FM Seattle, Rockline, Triple J Radio (Australia), WMXM 88.9FM Chicago, Self Pollution Radio.

We would like to thank the following photographers and picture agencies for supplying photographs: All Action: Justin Thomas/All Action; Suzan Moore/All Action; Gamma Liaison/Frank Spooner: Arnaldo Magnani/Gamma Liaison/Frank Spooner;

B. King/Gamma Liaison/Frank Spooner; S.I.N: JANA/S.I.N; Steve Double/S.I.N; Pentti Hokkanen/S.I.N; Frederick/JANA/S.I.N; NGI/S.I.N; Richard Beland/S.I.N; Soren Rud/ Alfa/Camera Press; Capital Pictures; *Melody Maker*; Retna Pictures: Adrian Green/Retna Pictures; Niels Van Iperen/Retna Pictures; Steve Eichner/Retna Pictures; Lance Mercer/ Retna Pictures; Lance Mercer/L.G.I/Retna Pictures; Jay Blakesberg/Retna Pictures; Armando Gallo/Retna Pictures; Fred Seaman/ Retna Pictures; Tony Mottram/Retna Pictures.

It has not been possible in all cases to trace the copyright sources, and the publishers would be glad to hear from any such unacknowledged copyright holders.

Special thanks to *Ferry Groen*. Also thanks to the excellent *Release Fanzine* site: www.release.org. Additional material supplied by Richard Porter, Tom Branton and Laura Coulman.

Cover photograph by Steve Gullick

'I feel like everybody else
in the band is a lot happier
with it than me.
Happy-go-lucky.
They kind of roll with it.
They enjoy it, even.
I can't seem to do that.
It's not that I think
I'm better than it.
I don't know.
I'm just not that happy
a person. I'm just not.
What I enjoy is seeing
music, getting to watch.
Watching Neil Young.
Or I get to watch
Sonic Youth from the side
of the stage.
That's what's been nice
for me . . .'

Eddie Vedder

CHAPTER ONE

MY REALITY

'My folks are very proud of me now, I'm thankful that they've given me a lifetime's worth of material to write about.'

Eddie

P rior to the winter of 1996, Eddie Vedder's childhood was generally perceived to have been a relatively simple, albeit somewhat dour affair. Famed for his verbosity on certain subjects, the millionaire lead singer of Pearl Jam had always become particularly uncommunicative when asked about his formative years. As Pearl Jam's popularity had grown, he had reluctantly let out snippets of information, allowing only a scratchy picture to be created, but one that suggested unhappiness. He was born Edward Louis Severson III, in late December 1964, the first of four sons of a doting mother, Marie. The family home was initially in Evanston, Illinois, but shortly after Eddie's third birthday the Muellers moved to San Diego in California. According to Eddie, his early years were emotionally barren,bereft of any meaningful relationship with the man he understood to be his biological father, a void which developed into open hostility as he grew up.

Money was always short and this affected Eddie's education. Such was his apparent dislike of school that, in interviews, Eddie has usually refused to discuss the subject, but it is clear that he struggled to keep up with the work and frequently fell foul of his teachers. 'They didn't treat me very well,' he told the *Los Angeles Times*. 'Well, maybe it was just that I wasn't going to like anybody because I had to work and I had to explain to my teachers why I wasn't keeping up.' His poor academic record was exacerbated by the atmosphere with his 'father' at home, which rapidly deteriorated to the point that when his parents moved back to Illinois just before Eddie's final school year, he stayed put in San Diego. When his mother and her husband left for Illinois, there was a heated and angry exchange and Eddie resolved never to speak to the man again – indeed, he never has.

Having to take menial jobs to support himself, including work at a Long's Drug Store in Encinitas, meant that Eddie's school work suffered even more: 'I'd fall asleep in class and they'd lecture me about the reality of their classroom,' Eddie recalled. 'I said, "You want to see my reality?" I opened up my backpack to where you usually keep your pencils. That's where I kept my bills . . . electric bills, rent . . . That was my reality.' As an added mark of rebellion he dropped his surname, Mueller, and took up his mother's maiden name, Vedder. His real father's name was Severson.

'Something made me realise it was time to get away or I was going to be just another loser.' *Eddie Vedder*

Almost inevitably Eddie dropped out of school. Work at the drugstore did little to ease the growing anger inside him, which was exacerbated by the spoilt kids who swanned into the shop: 'I resented everybody around who drove up in a car that someone provided for them . . . with insurance that someone provided for them,' he said. 'I'd be underneath some shelf putting price tags on tomato soup and I'd watch them come in . . . obnoxious with their fucking prom outfits on, buying condoms and being loud about it. I'd think, "Those fucks." Maybe I would have been doing that too, if the circumstances were different. Maybe that would have made me more forgiving, but I wasn't very forgiving at all. Everything was just such a fucking struggle for years.'

Eddie also revealed how near to self-destruction he came during this low period, when he talked of having thoughts of suicide 'as often as mealtime . . . I was all alone – except for music.'

This fascination with music had developed at an early age, but it wasn't until his teens that he really became hooked. At that time, his obsession was the Who's classic rock mock-opera, *Quadrophenia*, which recounted a compelling tale of disaffected youth that Eddie related to completely. Such was Eddie's fixation with this and other work by the Who that he later declared he 'should be sending Pete Townshend a card for Father's Day'. When Eddie began trying to create his own material, he found he had a rich seam of inspiration: 'My folks are very proud of me now,' he told *Rolling Stone*. 'I'm thankful that they've given me a lifetime's worth of material to write about.'

According to the accepted truth, a sixteen-year-old Eddie then embroiled himself in some less than savoury circles, supposedly dabbling with drugs and espousing a drop-out lifestyle, symptomatic of his utter rejection of parental constraints. But with a foresight that hinted at his exceptional instinct, Eddie managed to pull himself out of this shadowy world before it obilterated him, and instead he started to get more actively involved in the music scene in and around San Diego. 'All of a sudden', he told the *Los Angeles Times,* 'the big night out is sitting in somebody's trailer, smoking something or getting hold of something to put up your nose . . . I was getting swallowed up in it, but something made me realise it was time to get away or I was going to be just another loser.'

Eddie's already fraught childhood was about to deal him another body blow. One day out of the blue, his mother visited him from Chicago with the express purpose of telling him that his despised father, whom Eddie called 'the lawyer fuck', was not his biological parent. His real father had divorced his mother when Eddie was just two. Perhaps even more shockingly, his real father was in fact a family friend whom he had met on several occasions, but who had died from multiple sclerosis when Eddie was just thirteen. The news opened up a Pandora's box of emotions – the initial relief at being told the man he hated and disrespected was not his father was rapidly and painfully replaced by the realisation that his actual father was already dead. Eddie had seen him in hospital in a wheelchair and on a handful of neighbourly occasions, but any opportunity to build a relationship with this man was gone forever. The news also meant, of course, that Eddie's three siblings were only half-brothers.

Eddie remembers the day clearly: 'There was a piano in the room,' he explained in *Rolling Stone*, 'and I remember really wishing I knew how to play a happy song. I was happy for about a minute, and then I came down . . . I had to deal with the anger of not being told sooner, not being told while he was alive. I was a big secret. Secrets are bad news. Secrets about adoption, any of that stuff. It's got to come out, don't keep it. It just gets bigger and darker and deeper and uglier and messy.'

The news brought yet more conflict with his family,

as relatives pointed out that his biological father had been an organist-vocalist who sang in restaurants and small clubs – 'That's where you get your talent from.' Eddie resented this sudden interest in his musical ambitions, which had been ridiculed up until now: 'I was like, "Fuck you." At the time . . . I didn't even know what the fuck was going on. I learned how to play guitar, saved all my money for equipment, and you're telling me that's where it came from? Some fucking broken-down old lounge act? Fuck you.' (A later meeting with his real father's cousin left Eddie much more relaxed about the whole difficult episode: 'The strange thing is that there are so many similarities between my father and I,' he told *Rolling Stone*. 'He had no impact on my life, but here I am . . . I'm proud of the guy now. I appreciate my heritage. I have a very deep feeling for him in my heart.')

At the time of this startling revelation, Eddie was said to have been leading an isolated and cheerless existence. He claimed to be living in a 'shitty neighbourhood', waiting tables, working the graveyard shift at a petrol station, and the midnight shift as security at an upmarket hotel. He found this last job the most bearable, as he could enjoy taking a bottle of wine up on to the roof where he would write songs, a luxury which he remembers as 'like preying on the rich'. The strained vocals and tortured lyrics that were to propel Eddie to worldwide fame in Pearl Jam were traditionally seen as a product of this bitter, grim youth. In the paucity of information, this was all that most people could get to know about Eddie's formative years.

All this was questioned when *Rolling Stone* published an article by three writers, John Colopinto, Eric Boehlert, and Matt Hendrickson, in late November 1996 entitled 'Who You Are? Pearl Jam's Eddie Vedder' and all hell broke loose. The basic premise of the article was that Eddie had fabricated much of his 'difficult' childhood, and that his public persona as a troubled rock star was merely a facade designed to capture the fans' imagination. The article, quoted at length here, appeared well researched and drew on many so-called 'friends' of Eddie's from that period, attempting in the process to debunk the established theory that Eddie had struggled through his early years. Revealing the name of his school to be the San Dieguito High (Eddie had always refused to divulge this), the article quoted several classmates who appeared confounded by Eddie's infamously miserabilist persona, strongly refuting claims that he was an unpopular and lonely teenager.

Things are looking up. Promo shot from 1992, with from left to right: Jeff Ament, Dave Abbruzzese, Eddie and Stone Gossard.

One named source, a schoolmate called Annette Szymanski-Gomez, told *Rolling Stone,* 'He was very popular, he was outgoing. He'd go out of his way to be nice to everyone.' Another friend told the writers, 'He was so nice to everyone and took time to chat. That's why I don't understand this stuff about him being miserable. He didn't seem miserable to me! He was so doggone cute.' A third girl was even more direct, saying, 'All the girls had a crush on him.' The article talks of fun childhood games and of a happy, smiling 'little Eddie Mueller' playing simple guitar tunes to his many friends.

The refutation of Eddie's accepted childhood myth did not stop there. The 'shitty neighbourhood' he talks of is revealed to be 'a solid middle-class neighbourhood' where his family had 'a nice house' with two floors, a trim garden and a piano. One former classmate remembered seeing a pretty, framed picture of a cute three-year-old Eddie, and another talks of his bit part as a smiling toddler in some TV commercial.

Rolling Stone dug even deeper, following the story right through high school. The article revealed Eddie's main passion at this stage to be acting rather than music, recounting how he was an avid member of the school drama class (his idol was Dustin Hoffman). It listed the various musicals and plays he took part in, including *Little Mary Sunshine*, *Bye Bye Birdie*, *Butterflies Are Free*, *Outward Bound* and *The World of Carl Sandburg*. Some of these later roles were as the lead, and in his final year Eddie was voted 'Most Talented Actor' in the school. The article does agree that Eddie and his stepfather did not get along, but cited evidence that he instead found a mentor and father figure in his drama teacher, the late Clayton Liggett, whose widow said 'Eddie was in school, he would come over to our house quite often and talk to Clayton about personal things . . . Clayton was always there for him.'

The article substantiated further that Eddie was far from being a loner, detailing a long and deep relationship with a girl called Liz Gumble, who was in the year below him. They had fallen for each other during rehearsals for a school play in 1981, and were so in love that when she went away on vacation a distraught Eddie attended school with a scarf of hers wrapped melodramatically around his neck. The article suggests that Gumble's split with him was the only real source of stress in Eddie's childhood – by all accounts, he was inconsolable and dropped out of his beloved drama class and all theatre productions.

Eddie was then said to have left high school to live in Chicago for two years, before returning to California's idyllic beach community at La Mesa, near San Diego, in 1984. Now firmly set on a musical rather than a thespian career, Eddie was absolutely calculating and meticulous about his ambitions, according to *Rolling Stone*, which alleged that the popular myth that he succeeded in spite of his circumstances is pure fiction. The article claims he was a well-known networker on the local music scene, hanging around all the key clubs, especially the Bacchanal, talking to bands, drinking with agents and managers, drawing flyers, helping the roadies and just generally immersing himself in everything to do with the business. Eddie became a regular at the San Diego clubs and seedy venues where up-and-coming bands played. He frequently sneaked a tape recorder in, amassing a huge collection of bootlegs in the process.

When local group Bad Radio placed an advert for a singer in the *San Diego Reader* Eddie had already compiled a notebook full of songs (many of which were written on his various graveyard-shift jobs). Eddie's demo tape, which included a cover of Bruce Springsteen's 'Atlantic City', won him an audition, where he sang cover versions of various songs, including the Rolling Stones' 'Paint It Black'. Bad Radio were flabbergasted by his charisma and enrolled him immediately; one band member told *Rolling Stone*, 'We were blown away.'

Eddie had once told how Bad Radio's debut show made him so nervous that he performed wearing goggles with blacked out lenses that prevented him from having to look at the audience. In *Rolling Stone*, however, far from being a shy performer hiding behind painted goggles, fellow music-scene friends remembered Eddie as an extrovert and consummate performer, raging around the stage, enigmatically captivating the crowd. Offstage, too, he was far from withdrawn, with the article claiming he rapidly took over Bad Radio, acting as their agent, manager and main songwriter – he even designed complex flyers and the demo cassette inlays. This enforced control, it was claimed, soon turned into total domination as Eddie focussed the band on the causes that he held dear to his heart: many of his songs already spoke of homelessness, poverty and the environment, and Eddie was only too keen for Bad Radio to be involved in charity for those causes. Quite often, the rest of the band would be left in the dark;

as bassist Dave Silva told *Rolling Stone,* 'He wouldn't let us get close enough to him to say we want to be a part of it. He'd just say, "We're doing this show and this benefit." He'd go out at Thanksgiving and buy all this food, feed homeless people. He'd tell us afterwards, and we'd be like, "Oh my God, we would have helped." He didn't really let us know what he was thinking.'

'He was constantly trying to put his band in some place where it could be seen.' *Tim Hall*

Bad Radio played a strange mix of styles, mixing funk, rock and even New Romantic pop in a peculiar and at times rather clumsy amalgam of sound. Eddie's vocals at this stage were far higher and more shrill than the deep anguished growl for which he would later become famous. With a Bad Radio demo in his hand, Eddie hustled hard – a well-known local club owner, Tim Hall, recounted to *Rolling Stone* how 'Eddie was constantly promoting that band, trying to make it into something' and a friend from the local scene, Steve Saint, continued, '90 percent of guys in garage bands are sitting around, waiting to be discovered, waiting for some record agent to knock on their door. Eddie didn't take that attitude. He was constantly trying to put his band in some place where it could be seen.'

Along the way, Eddie met scores of past and future stars, hanging out with people like the Red Hot Chili Peppers, the Sugarcubes, the Clash's Joe Strummer and former Police drummer Stewart Copeland. Usually wearing green shorts and combat boots, Eddie ingratiated himself with many of the bands who would later be his musical peers, in the process becoming well versed in the pitfalls of making a band breakthrough. In addition to the pop stars he met, his long-time girlfriend, Beth Liebling, was also heavily involved in the music business, first as a booker at San Diego State University, then at Virgin Records. Between them, Eddie and Beth proved to be a formidable team, and the degree to which they seemed to know everyone was displayed with the ease with which they later promoted a weekly gothic rock show called 'Red Tape' at Winters, a favourite student haunt.

During his time in Bad Radio, Eddie befriended Saifudinov, the manager at the studio where they rehearsed. He had started the first rock band in Russia, and according to *Rolling Stone*, the two became close friends. Saifudinov feels it may have been his own strict ethics about music that imbued Eddie with the principles that flourished so strongly later in his career: 'We had a mutual sympathy for each other. I was eighteen or nineteen years older than him, but it didn't feel like it . . . I would say to him, "First you're a musician. You're a songwriter. That's what counts. Any idiot can put a salami in his pants and pose. Or become an asshole because you have money."'

Pearl Jam's dour reputation started early on.

Amongst the various gigs that Bad Radio played were benefit shows for Amnesty International, various rain forest charities, and homeless groups. Eddie always went a little bit further though – one day he was seen with just an acoustic guitar outside a local council meeting, singing Tracy Chapman's 'Talkin' Bout A Revolution' while the politicians inside talked about low-income housing. *Rolling Stone* also accounts with relish how Eddie and Beth once took in a homeless man, bathed and dressed him and paid for him to go back to his home in the Midwest, leaving Eddie to muse over the polaroids they had taken of the transformation.

Unfortunately, a void opened up between Eddie and the other members of Bad Radio, and the former's increasing involvement in social issues proved to be the undoing of the group. By late 1989, it had become clear that Bad Radio were no longer supplying Eddie with the zeal he needed, and three years after passing that first audition, he left. Backstage at the Bacchanal, Eddie tellingly gave Saifudinov his reason: 'I just have to move on. I'm trying to go and do things.'

The *Rolling Stone* article's allegations were substantiated by several other details. Eddie himself had always been vague and elusive about his childhood, and when asked directly he often became aggressive and surly. On one occasion he seemed to retreat entirely, saying, 'I'm confused . . I'm mixed up about everything. I don't know what's happening.' Also, other sources appeared saying that the idea of the miserable, tortured Eddie was, as the article said, in complete contrast to the friend they had known. Rob Jensen, another musician, worked as a temporary accountant at the Chevron petrol station where Eddie worked the late shift, and he wrote in the *San Diego Reader* how he always felt Eddie was friendly, approachable and contented. He talked of his 'friendly smile'. He went on: 'He was funny and outgoing.' Girls in the office thought he was cute. And they liked his short hair . . . He was a great storyteller. I'm not sure, though, if the stories he told were entirely true.' Eddie apparently bragged of Hollywood parties he had been to and pop stars he had met, including the comical time he had bumped into one of the actors from *The Brady Bunch* and had asked, 'So where's Bobby? Fucking Cindy?'

Jensen recalled how Eddie loved telling his stories from the Bacchanal, all about Bad Radio and their hopes, and remembers being taken aback by Eddie's drive: 'He seemed so happy to be doing what he was doing. Once I asked him what he wanted to do with his life. He said he wanted to do music, to be a professional musician, and to go "all the way". A sarcastic "Good luck" went through my mind.' Jensen scoffed at these ambitions and admitted he thought his own cover band had far more potential than one that played original compositions that no-one knew ('I was convinced I could get more girls by singing songs they were familiar with'). Eddie invited him over to jam one night, but the

PEARL JAM · NONE TOO FRAGILE

16

offer was politely forgotten.

Even so, when Jensen saw Eddie on the television as the weary, anguished lead singer of Pearl Jam, he was a little surprised: 'Who was this quiet, frowning person in the magazines and on TV? The Eddie I vaguely remembered was a funny, outgoing, smiling guy. This person was angry, hushed, distant, wearing a constant expression of grave concern. He sang in agony, in grungy clothes, arms folded across his chest. In interviews he expressed deep disappointment with his success and with life in general, often barely able to complete a sentence without struggling to find the words. Since then, I've come to realise I probably didn't know him as well as I thought.'

It is this last comment that is the most telling. Although *Rolling Stone*'s article was revealing, it mentioned little about Eddie's parental bombshell, nor did it explain why it was such a betrayal for a pop star to deliberately court and pursue success (are rock stars valid only if they stumble across fame, and just how many actually do this?). Obviously, if the sources were to be believed, then there was a side to Eddie's childhood that he had not wished to reveal, and there was some evidence that his anti-establishment rock star persona was not completely truthful. However, the tabloid-style mockery in the article meant it was as much an exercise in discrediting Eddie as a pure piece of investigative journalism. *Rolling Stone*, tired of being denied access to the singer through Pearl Jam's press bans, had gone for the jugular.

When asked about the article, Eddie claimed not to have read it, although he admitted some friends had told him of the allegations. He replied to them in the *Los Angeles Times*: 'I know who I am, and I don't need to read someone else's bitter take on it.' He continued, 'If I was all that popular, I am just finding out about it now. I must have had a bunch of friends I didn't even know about . . . I don't think that was the case. It must just be so many people now saying they were my friends.' Several prominent celebrities, including Courtney Love, Michael Stipe and Tim Robbins, chastised *Rolling Stone* for the piece in angry letters to the editor. Unfortunately, in many senses, the damage was done. Having said that, this article was just another in a long line of negative attacks on Eddie and his band that Pearl Jam have had to endure. Not that this has stopped them from being successful . . .

CHAPTER TWO

NEWS FROM THE NORTHWEST

'In terms of communicating we were a pretty dysfunctional band. There was a lot of intimidation going on, and we were four strong personalities trying to outmanoeuvre one another.'

Jeff

Back when a thirteen-year-old Eddie was blasting the Who from his stereo, a strange and ultimately historical phenomenon was developing several hundred miles north of San Diego, in the Pacific northwestern tip of the United States. Over the years, this area of the country had nurtured a handful of internationally revered musical acts, most obviously Jimi Hendrix, but also credible underground acts such as the Sonics, the Fleetwoods, and a sprinkling of more mainstream artists such as Robert Cray, Heart, Kenny G, Quincy Jones and Queensryche. However, these successes were sporadic and isolated, with no thread of association between the respective artists.

Back in 1979, with punk still lingering on and Sid Vicious fresh in his grave, a fanzine entitled *Subterranean Pop* emerged in Olympia, Washington. Compiled by Illinois native Bruce Pavitt, the fanzine focussed on alternative American music from across the country. Starting with the 200 copies of the first edition, the fanzine established itself, in the process moving to Seattle and shortening its name to *Sub Pop*. Shortly after this, Pavitt decided to improve on the free cassette which accompanied some issues by releasing some vinyl. Thus in 1986, *Sub Pop 100* was released, including tracks by Sonic Youth, Steve Fisk, the U-Men, Steve Albini and Skinny Puppy. Towards the end of that year, Kim Thayil of Soundgarden introduced Pavitt to another underground music impresario, Jonathan Poneman, who possessed the crucial ingredient that he lacked – money. After some initial reluctance, the two formed a partnership, and the combination of their skills proved to be enormously successful.

Their first release was by a band called Green River. Led by Stone Gossard and Jeff Ament, Green River had already had a track released on a compilation called *DeepSix,* on the C/Z label back in 1985. Gossard in many ways was the epitome of what was to become known as the Seattle sound. Born and raised in that city, he was as rooted in the region as any of his contemporaries. Ironically, unlike the dysfunctional backgrounds that so many of his future peers came from, Gossard's family life was very comfortable. His father was a well-heeled and reputable attorney, and his mother worked for the city government. The family home was a substantial house in a middle-class neighbourhood and his parents' marriage remained solid. Furthermore, his artistic leanings were encouraged when he was sent to the progressive Northwestern School of the Arts. It was here that he was able to develop his rapidly growing guitar skills, learned mostly from seventies' rock acts like Kiss, Led Zeppelin, AC/DC, Queen and Boston, as well as Hendrix and some African-American styles. The latter years of that decade also introduced him to punk rock through the local bands who had been influenced by it, so somewhat belatedly he found himself inspired by the likes of Johnny Thunders and the Sex Pistols. He told *Guitar Player* magazine, 'It was all loud guitars. None of those guys could really play. I was around sixteen years old, and I said, "I'm going to get a guitar and start a band right off the bat." That's how you did it. There was no training or anything. You got right into it.'

'Players like Johnny Thunders were incredibly inspiring because they . . . were just bad-ass. What they were singing about, their image, and what they represented said, "You don't need to be Tom Scholz to be in a band." That's why punk is so great: it inspired a lot of people to pick up guitars. It was what it must have been like when rock happened the first time. There was no precedent of these phenomenal, technical players. It was all about the groove, dancing, and having a good time. Punk rock was the key to me feeling comfortable going out and saying, "I can do that."'

After starting off in various minor acts, including one called the Ducky Boys, Gossard formed Green River in the mid-eighties with Montana born Jeff Ament. After moving from Havre to Big Sandy as a toddler, Ament had always felt suffocated by the claustrophobic atmosphere in his hometown. With intensely religious parents (in an intensely religious place), in a town with a population of only 800 and no music store, Ament's teenage years were very frustrating. When he ventured to the nearest record shop in nearby Great Fall, he found the proprietor rarely stocked rock records. Although he learned to play the piano from first grade, Ament tired of it (he had to pay for his lessons by mowing the teacher's lawn) and hankered after something more exciting. At first he found the answer not in rock music but in sports, particularly basketball and football.

By fifth grade, he had started to take a shine to the records his trendy uncle played him during weekend family visits. The uncle often gave him singles he no longer wanted, including records by the Beatles, Simon and Garfunkel, Santana and Ted Nugent. 'I thought Uncle Pat was one of the coolest people in the universe,' Ament later told *Bass Player* magazine. 'He had long hair and sideburns, and his room had candles all over the place and Santana posters on the walls. I probably got as excited about hanging out with my uncle as I did about anything.'

'That's why punk is so great: it inspired a lot of people to pick up guitars.' *Steve Gossard*

Soon after, Ament bought a Gibson SG copy and tried learning the guitar, but after only a couple of months he gave up and returned to his beloved basketball, which now took up much of his spare time. In fact, music was only third in Ament's interests, also following his talent at art, of which his parents were notably supportive. When he was eighteen, he started an art course at the University of Montana in Missoula, which ironically turned him back on to music. He teamed up with a fellow undergraduate and Black Flag fan and formed a band but once more he felt suffocated by the local surroundings, and Ament came to the conclusion that he had to leave Montana in order to experience life more fully. Spurred on by the excitement he felt whenever his family went on their hard-earned annual vacations to Los Angeles or Minneapolis, he moved to Seattle along with his friend. Within a week of moving, they had seen concerts by the Clash, the Who and X.

It was at a Seattle club called the Metropolis that Ament first met Stone Gossard, as well as two other musicians called Mark Arm and Steve Turner, who had both played in the Limp Richards and Mr Epp. Ament's own band, Deranged Diction, played some support slots to Husker Dü, DOA and the Butthole Surfers, but after less than a year Ament grew disillusioned and the band split up. Now a free agent, he was approached by Arm and Turner to form a band, who also recruited Deranged Diction's Bruce Fairweather as an extra guitarist, and Alex Vincent from Spluii Numa on drums. They took the band's name from a local waterway renowned for its associations with a serial killer: Green River.

Once Gossard was in the line-up, things started to hot up for Green River. Turner and Arm were seasoned and ardently anti-commercial musicians, so the newly-formed band were soon snapped up by the small indie label, Homestead Records. Unfortunately, their debut record took so long to release that the band had already returned (broke) from the tour to promote it before it appeared. Nevertheless, this tour had won them critical praise and, shortly after, Sub Pop's Bruce Pavitt called them up with the offer of a new record deal. An agreement was made, and Sub Pop's first record, Green River's 'Dry As A Bone', was recorded.

In many senses Green River were the pioneers of the Seattle sound, and one of the very first of the so-called 'grunge' bands, touting a raucous mix of punk and hard-edged rock. They toured widely along the West Coast, including filling a support slot to Perry Farrell's seminal Jane's Addiction, and garnered a strong underground following in the process. Unfortunately Green River was fraught with differences, and a couple of personnel changes did little to stabilise the problems of what was always an unlikely blend of musicians. Musically, Mark Arm played far from easy-listening punk, whilst Stone Gossard and Jeff Ament were increasingly venturing into solid rock sounds. Ethically there were problems too – Arm, in particular, was so fervently anti-commercial that his principles and goals were constantly clashing with those of the rather more careerist Ament and Gossard. Inevitably, this polarity appeared more and more often, until Green River could no longer operate effectively. On Hallowe'en 1987, they split up, ironically just before their debut album *Rehab Doll* was released by Sub Pop. 'We were five guys playing five different things,' Arm recollected. 'It worked for a while, and then it didn't.' Arm and Turner left to form the highly

Jeff Ament's love of playing music is matched by his passion for basketball.

respected and anti-establishment Mudhoney, whilst Gossard, Fairweather and Ament had more mainstream ideas in mind.

Inspired by Jane's Addiction's limited technical prowess but extraordinary creative talent, the three ex-Green River men teamed up with vocalist and general oddball Andrew Wood (former frontman and bass player of the quirky Malfunkshun, a band he formed with his brother). Recruiting drummer Greg Gilmore (formerly of Ten Minute Warning, which also featured future Guns N' Roses guitarist Duff McKagan), the new band had a decidedly

'We were five guys playing five different things. It worked for a while, and then it didn't.' *Mark Arm*

glam noise-rock sound. They called themselves Mother Love Bone. Andrew Wood was a highly enigmatic character, often going under the moniker of 'L'andrew, the love child', and was a peculiar performer. *The Rocket* magazine reviewed one Mother Love Bone concert thus: 'On stage an obdurate rhythm line, best described as a mongrel amalgamation of punk and funk, forms the fabric for the melody, which two guitars lace together in a psychedelic Middle Eastern flamenco. The singer has just anointed the faithful with the contents of his beer glass, his pouty outrageousness, balanced on the edge of pretension, is focused in his hiss . . . Lewd, loose, and lascivious, the entire assemblage proceeds to jump, thrust and howl for the next 45 minutes until neither the band nor the audience has another ounce of energy to drain from each other. This pandemonium is more or less your typical evening with Mother Love Bone.'

The new band played many covers, but also aired much of the material that Gossard and Ament had felt too suffocated to play in Green River. Over the top of all this was Wood's glam shock vocals and bizarre personality. The powerful combination created something of an A&R frenzy in the Northwest, such that Mother Love Bone found themselves being scouted by several major labels. Such was the interest that before one show (where Capitol, Island, Atlantic, A&M, PolyGram and Geffen were all present) a record company executive approached them and said, 'You don't need to talk to those other people – we'll give you $300,000 right now.' The band's manager, Kelly Curtis, recalls in the *Rocket* how the situation had quickly escalated out of control: 'There was some initial excitement about the band and then everybody else jumped on the bandwagon. Suddenly people were flying up here to take the band to dinner who had no idea, no clue, as to what the band was about. They heard . . . I don't know what, and I don't even know why they flew up here, but this was not the type of band that going to sign with the big schmooze guy.' After this rather tasteless scramble for their signatures, the band finally plumped for PolyGram in November 1989, reportedly signing a seven-album deal with an advance of over a quarter of a million dollars. This was the first time that the majors had taken notice of the blossoming Seattle scene, although it had been incredibly productive for some years by then. Soundgarden signed a deal with A&M shortly after.

Earmarked as 'the next big thing' the pressure was on Mother Love Bone to produce a strong debut album, not least to recoup the enormous sums already advanced. Were they the most sellable version of this so-called 'Seattle sound', or would they prove to be just another sterile addition to the Guns N' Roses school of arena rock? The pressure was increased by tensions within the group, as Ament told *Bass Player* magazine: 'In terms of communicating we were a pretty dysfunctional band. There was a lot of intimidation going on, and we were four strong personalities trying to outmanoeuvre one another.' The stakes were raised still further by the posthumous success, both critical and popular, of Green River's debut album, *Rehab Doll*. Despite all these distractions, they managed to record the much-anticipated debut release, *Apple*, during a productive Thanksgiving studio session, and prepared themselves for the album tour. Then, just before the planned release, Andrew Wood died from a heroin overdose.

For Ament, this was a devastating blow, not just because he had lost a friend. From a musical point of view, after years of trying, they had finally got into a position that most bands can only dream about: 'I strongly considered never playing again, because I had worked so hard to get to that point, only to have it all taken away. I didn't feel like starting over. But I had quit college and didn't know what I was supposed to do with my life.' Mother Love Bone was finished.

Mike McCready is obviously not gifted at picking band names – two of his first efforts were called Warrior and Shadow. Fortunately, he was far more talented at playing the guitar. The Florida-born only child of a primary school art teacher and civil servant, he displayed early signs of a musical bent by playing his father's bongos while listening incessantly to Hendrix and Santana. As with Ament, Kiss had a big effect on McCready and proved to be the catalyst for him to buy his first guitar, a Les Paul copy which he bought from the local music store (an instrument that he still owns to this day).

After taking some lessons and annoying his father with dire versions of 'Smoke On The Water', McCready formed his first band, the afore-mentioned Warrior, who transformed into the equally dreadfully named Shadow. Rather than the spandex-clad soft-rock their name suggested, Shadow were more rooted in the harder rock of Ozzy Osbourne, Black Sabbath and Thin Lizzy. Once he had left high school, McCready felt confident enough to head for Los Angeles to plug the band, and, taking residence near Melrose Avenue, he took a job in Aron's Records. Thirteen months and countless poorly attended gigs later, Shadow admitted defeat and headed back home. 'We played to a couple bartenders down there,' McCready told *Guitar Player* magazine, 'But even though it was a bad scene, it was a good experience. Basically, we weren't that great a band, and we didn't realise it until we got down there. I guess we lost our focus, got really bummed out and came back to Seattle.' Shadow split up six months later, in mid-1988.

Disillusioned, McCready almost gave up on his music altogether. He enrolled at a local community college and cut his hair into a tidy crop, leaving his guitar to gather dust in his room. He supported himself by working at a video store, where he sat depressed all day, reading texts by the ultra-right wing former Republican presidential candidate, Barry Goldwater. Eventually, his close friend Russ Riedner had had enough, and began coaxing McCready back to music with a loose band called Love Chile, which was heavily influenced by Stevie Ray Vaughan and other electric blues guitarists. McCready was happy to plod along with this arrangement until one day at a party, whilst jamming away to a Stevie Ray Vaughan record on a borrowed amplifier, he bumped into Stone Gossard, whom he had known before either of them had played music. As he was a fan of Mother Love Bone,

McCready was extremely flattered when Gossard told him he loved his guitar playing. About three months later, Gossard got back in touch and asked McCready if he wanted to jam with a new line-up. Gossard had a feeling McCready fitted the bill. His instinct was vindicated as soon as he saw Love Chile perform live: 'Whatever you're playing, Cready comes in and lights the fuse.' McCready had left the video store job, and was now working in a restaurant called Julia's in north Seattle, hardly the most exciting of career moves, so when Gossard asked him to join the new band officially, he jumped at the chance.

The two reunited friends jammed endlessly in the attic of Gossard's parents' house, where so much of the material for Green River and Mother Love Bone had been created. McCready told *Guitar Player* magazine how he found working with Gossard instantly inspiring: 'Stone and I just clicked together, he had tons of songs – the beginnings of 'Alive' and 'Black' – and I was like, "Shit, yeah!" Our guitars really complemented each other; his sense of melody and rhythm, my lead style.' He also said to *Rolling Stone*, 'I knew we had a band when we started playing that song 'Dollar Short'.'

Meanwhile, in the wake of Wood's death Jeff Ament had been keeping his hand in with two informal bands, War Babies and Love Co., but, despite initial reservations, he and Gossard agreed to start working together again. Ament described what happened: 'I played on a friend's demo and found it to be easy and fun, and Stone started writing some more songs. But there were some things he and I needed to talk about before we could play together again. We went to dinner and decided we needed to communicate more. We had been playing together for years and had developed an unspoken musical connection, but I felt if we took our personal relationship to another level, that would take our music to another level too. So we aired a lot of the negative feelings we had about each other and that's how we got through Andy's death and started putting things together again.' With Dallas scenester Dave Krusen agreeing to fill in on drums, the line-up of a new band was almost complete. The question was, who would they get on vocals?

CHAPTER THREE

THE OUTSIDER ON VOCALS

'My relationship with the band began as a love affair on the phone with Jeff.'

Eddie

All these complex and layered band developments were, of course, completely outside the world of Eddie Vedder. Pumping gas by night and surfing or hanging out at his girlfriend's Mission Beach house in the day, Eddie was becoming increasingly isolated. Most days he would try to write and record music, and on his nights off he would work for nothing as a roadie in local clubs, 'Just to be closer to the whole pulse of what was going on.' He only had a handful of close friends, including Jack Irons, who drummed with the Red Hot Chili Peppers and occasionally played basketball with him. Jack knew of Eddie's musical aspirations, especially as he was such a well-known face on the San Diego scene, and he was impressed by what he had heard of his work. So when his friend Stone Gossard mentioned he was actively looking for a singer, Irons immediately recommended Eddie, who after a couple of phone-calls, travelled to Seattle to meet up. Eddie liked Gossard and his friends but obviously had to hear what they were playing first, so he travelled back to San Diego with a copy of a demo tape marked 'Stone Gossard Demo '91' in his pocket. It was late September 1990.

The demo consisted of tracks which the fresh line-up of Gossard, Ament, McCready and Krusen had recorded the previous month, during sessions which they christened 'the Gossman Project'. Gossard and Ament had already shopped the tape around to various record business associates, including the Wilder Brothers, but it was the sample of the full session, including 'Alive', 'Once', 'Footsteps', 'Black' and 'Alone', that found them their vocalist.

Known endearingly by locals as 'the man who never slept', due to his anti-social shifts and his preference for surf over catching up on shut-eye, Eddie was on the wrong end of a particularly sleep-deprived few days when the tape landed in his lap. After playing the songs and instrumentals over many times at work, he went back home to bed, but awoke the next day to find the material going round and round his head. In order to mull over his reaction, Eddie took to the surf: 'The sleep deprivation came into play,' he said in *Rolling Stone*. 'You get so sensitive that it feels like every nerve is directly exposed . . . I was literally writing some of these words as I was going up against a wave or paddling.'

Racing from the water back to the beach house, Eddie scribbled down lyrics that had come to him in a flourish onto dozens of yellow 'Post It' notes he had stolen from work. Then he recorded himself over three of the instrumentals that Gossard had put on tape – 'Dollar Short', 'Once' and 'Footsteps' (the first of which had started life during Gossard's Mother Love Bone days and was later renamed 'Alive'). With admirable confidence, Eddie marked his vocal tapes 'Mamasan', xeroxed some graphics he had designed himself, then sent his efforts off straight away. 'I didn't really know what Stone and Jeff wanted', Eddie told *Rip* magazine. 'The music just felt really open to me. Then I thought, "Wow, the music is really good; maybe I should have paid more attention. Maybe I should have written it down. Maybe I should have really listened to it before I sent it off."'

Eddie need not have worried. Tired of the endless stream of Andrew Wood sound-and-look-alikes they had been auditioning, Gossard and Ament were beginning to wonder where their new singer was going to come from. When they had met Eddie, they were pleased to see he knew nothing about Mother Love Bone or Andrew Wood, but what was his singing like? Playing Eddie's tape in his Seattle apartment, Jeff Ament was flabbergasted. He picked up the phone and called Gossard: 'Stone, you'd better get over here.'

• • •

What Eddie had committed to tape was a weird, disturbing mini-opera. The rambling triumvirate of tracks told a seedy and unsettling story of one man's slide into violence, insanity and finally death. The opening track was 'Alive', the first act so to speak. This told of a widowed mother who finds herself drawn sexually towards her son, who bears a remarkable physical similarity to her late husband. The resulting incestuous atmosphere starts to unhinge the son, and his mental stability crumbles. The next act, the track called 'Once', details the violent rage the situation evoked in him, a psychological anguish which he expressed by becoming a grisly and ultra-violent serial killer. The closing act, the song 'Times of Trouble' (later changed to 'Footsteps'), ends with the son in a jail cell, contemplating his own execution and all the death he has caused. Gossard called it 'a kind of a sick, disturbed rock opera – if Nietzsche were to write a rock opera . . .'

Although all three tracks were startling, it was undoubtedly 'Alive' that was the most striking. Eddie later denied that it was autobiographical, but at the same time admitted there were elements that were drawn directly from his own experience: 'I started dealing with a few things that I hadn't dealt with,' he told *Rolling Stone*. 'It was great music – it was bringing things out of me that hadn't been brought out.'

'When I first heard the tape I couldn't believe it; it sounded like he had written the songs with us.' Suitably impressed, Gossard and Ament invited Eddie up to Seattle to rehearse. Eddie readily agreed but only on the condition that he meet them at the studio straight off the plane – during his lengthy conversations on the phone before he had received the tape, he had expressed the wish that no-one's time be wasted. He arrived clutching a lyric sheet for a song which would evolve into 'Black' and plunged into the rehearsal studio. They set up and began playing 'Alive', which proved to be the start of a remarkably creative time, playing non-stop for ten hours on that day alone. The following week was crammed with similarly intense and lengthy sessions, and within a matter of days they had written three new songs (including 'Deep' and 'Jeremy') with Eddie producing completed lyrics to add to a further three instrumentals.

On the fifth day of that week they recorded some of those songs on a demo, and the following day they played their first show (22 September 1990). Some of the tapes they had sent out to prospective venues were accompanied by an NBA trading card of a New Jersey Nets basketball player, whom Gossard and Ament liked because he was a perennial underdog. Many venues called them up to book a gig and assumed that the player's monicker, Mookie Blaylock, was the band's name, and so, for a time, it became. Even at this early stage, there was a buzz on the Seattle grapevine about the new incarnation, with special interest in the outsider on vocals: 'I just remember hearing about this amazing, intense singer,' Kim Warnick of the Seattle punk band Fastbacks told *Rolling Stone*. 'The band was soon getting line-ups around the block.' For everyone concerned, the speed and effortless manner in which the new line-up had emerged with such a glut of quality material was of almost a spiritual magnitude: 'It was just a totally magical thing,' says Eddie. 'It was the most intense musical experience I'd ever been involved in.'

Eddie returned to San Diego for a few weeks to tie up some loose ends before relocating to Seattle on a permanent basis. More shows were already planned, including an invaluable support slot with Alice In Chains, which gave the new band a vital push start. Although it has been claimed that Mookie Blaylock loved the name and was a big fan, others say the player complained and forced them to rethink their title. Whatever the reason, his feelings reinforced the new group's own reservations. There was the feeling within the band that the name would not be taken seriously by major labels. Eddie had mentioned that his grandmother Pearl was married to a native Indian, who was heavily into hallucinogens and peyote. She knew of a closely guarded secret recipe to make strongly hallucinogenic preserves. Suitably inspired, Mookie Blaylock, after only a dozen or so gigs, duly re-christened themselves Pearl Jam.

• • •

While all this had been going on, something remarkable had been happening in Seattle. The talk of the 'sound of Seattle' was now whistling around the world's music papers, and increasing attention was being paid to Northwest bands, especially Nirvana. Sub Pop was suddenly the trendiest record label in the world, and A&R men from all the majors were regularly cropping up in Seattle clubs unannounced. The great hopes for Nirvana's forthcoming album *Nevermind*, and the plethora of quality acts from in or around the region was whipping up interest. Soundgarden enjoyed great success with their heavily rock-based material on *Superunknown*, and bands like Alice In Chains, and the more underground likes of Tad and Mudhoney, were all given a higher profile. Before long, every so-called 'loser' kid had a pair of combat boots, wore a lumberjack shirt and long hair, and carried a copy of Nirvana's little-known first album *Bleach*, claiming to have owned it since its release. Kurt Cobain and Nirvana were the undoubted spiritual heads of this movement, as far as the kids were concerned, but fairly soon their position in the commercial stakes would be challenged by Pearl Jam. With the media and corporate seizure of all things Seattle, the term 'grunge' was christened, and for the next two years it ruled the world.

• • •

Another interesting development from the blossoming Seattle scene was the film *Singles*, directed by Cameron Crowe and featuring members of Pearl Jam as well as Alice In Chains and Soundgarden. Crowe was a big fan of Green River and Soundgarden, and while first developing the idea mentioned it to Gossard and Ament one night. Crowe's idea was to chronicle the life of a fictitious Seattle band, Citizen Dick, in and around the underground scene. With Matt Dillon on lead vocals, Crowe already had his big-name actor, but interestingly he chose to cast Ament on bass, Gossard on guitar and Eddie Vedder on drums! The rumours were that Dillon's womanising and selfishness were based on Ament, but the latter liked to think he wasn't all that bad, telling the *Seattle Times*: 'He's more based on the type of things I've done. He works in a coffee place, it shows him screening T-shirts and doing a lot of the band's artwork. But his love interest and the way he goes about it, that's not me.' *Singles* was effectively a *Saturday Night Fever* for the grunge generation, featuring a whole host of now-famous rockers, including a performance by Soundgarden. Needless to say, the film fared very well at the box office.

• • •

While Eddie was auditioning for the band that became Pearl Jam, two of its members were involved in another side project, called Temple Of The Dog. The inspiration for this band started off as a veiled tribute to Andrew Wood. Temple Of The Dog was an idea of Chris Cornell's of Soundgarden, a close friend of Wood's, who had lived with him through some of his most difficult times. Cornell heard the news of his death shortly before flying off on tour, and found that far from easing his grief by being away from Seattle, the transient lifestyle worsened matters by offering him little or no means to vent his feelings. Faced with a grim hotel wall each night, and desperate to articulate his emotions, Cornell started writing songs.

'The songs I wrote weren't really stylistically like something my band Soundgarden would be used to playing or would be natural for us to do,' Cornell told KISW 99.9 FM Radio in Seattle, 'but it was material that Andy really would have liked, so I didn't really want to just throw it out the window or put it away in a box,

Image really matters when you've just formed a new band. Even in Pearl Jam's early days, Eddie is clearly taking centre stage.

y'know, put the tape away and never listen to it again.' So on his return Cornell enquired of Gossard and Ament if they wished to be involved in an informal band to record this new material. While there were a few grumblings of discontent from Wood's family and a girlfriend, his former band colleagues Gossard and Ament were delighted to have been asked and agreed straight away. The line-up was completed by Soundgarden's drummer Matt Cameron.

Cornell saw the Wood family's misgivings as 'totally fair, but it wasn't something that any of us felt like having to explain or worry about, so we decided we would make our own album, let the Andrew thing go, and have fun collaborating as a band, because we were really having a good time working together. The rest of the material came within a few weeks.'

Although the emphasis of the project was not now a direct tribute to Wood, some of the tracks touched on issues that had dominated his life. 'Reach Down' talked about the contradiction of wanting to be famous whilst simultaneously being terrified of performing. This was a paradox that Cornell knew Wood struggled with, but it also created a dynamic that proved enormously creative: 'When he died, I felt really hollow, really lonely. When he was alive, I felt I was part of something that was really vital and really cool and really different. When he was gone, it was like, "It was my responsibility." It was a real serious absence. A lot of people helped bring me out of that, like Layne from Alice In Chains, and Eddie, Pearl Jam's singer – he's a great guy. That really helped.'

Eddie became involved when Cornell saw him trying out for Pearl Jam and was instantly impressed. Eddie's personality and remarkable voice seemed ideal for the project: 'He was at one of our rehearsals . . . and he told me afterwards that he really liked one of the songs which wasn't really the way I was used to singing, and I thought his voice suited that song really well and I thought it would be great to do a duet.' Cornell continued, 'He sang half of that song not even knowing that I'd wanted the part to be there and he sang it exactly the way I was thinking about doing it, just instinctively . . .' Eddie also provided back-up vocals on three other songs, and even though he had never met Wood, Cornell remembers he was delighted to join in: 'Yeah, when I asked him, it seemed like he was flattered, it wasn't anything any of us had planned. He was just there and he's a great guy and an amazing singer, and I was like, "this is a fun project, so why not have him involved as well?"'

The one-off band recorded fifteen songs in three weeks, for the eponymous album (not all of them were used). Also on *Temple Of The Dog* was a track called 'Times Of Trouble', which was Cornell's version of the Gossard instrumental that Eddie had turned into 'Footsteps'. The collection of songs on the album was not written specifically for, or about, Andrew Wood, but was unified by a heavy, mournful atmosphere. A gig was played at Seattle's Off Ramp club, and Cornell and Cameron later performed a few of the songs at a Pearl Jam gig. The band also released a single ('Hunger Strike', with a video), to complement the album's considerable sales success (it later reached a platinum-selling position of Number 5 in the *Billboard* charts),but the project was never going to be a long-term effort. Temple Of The Dog's own biography on the album sleeve probably best sums up what they were doing: '10 songs. Spontaneous. Creation. Emotion. Very Pleasing. Real Music. No Analyzation. No Pressure. No Hype. Just music to make music. Friends and a reason. Chemistry. Beauty. Life Rules!'

• • •

Even at this early stage there were grumbles of discontent about the sudden and potentially explosive arrival of Pearl Jam on the Seattle scene. Although the band had barely started, one key reason was that some local musicians resented the selection of outsider Eddie Vedder over the dozens of struggling hopefuls in the city. Eddie set about putting this right immediately; he started working himself into the network around Seattle, and attended gigs and parties constantly. Kim Warnick found Eddie waiting for her backstage after one Fastbacks show, where he flooded her with compliments. The next day she received a fan letter from him and his girlfriend Beth signed in glitter. She told *Rolling Stone*: 'It's actually real, when he talks to you, it's like you're the only person in the room. He leans close, and he's frowning and real intense.' Her willingness to befriend Eddie paid off when Pearl Jam later offered her band support slots on one of their world tours.

Furthermore, there were derisory whispers about the acknowledged careerism of Gossard and Ament. It was no secret that this had been at the very core of Green River's break-up, and to the alternative music fascists obsessed with 'credibility', this was a serious discredit to the band. 'From the beginning,' continued Warnick, 'they were defined by their audience, which wasn't punk. They were the "bogus" suburban rock kids.'

For now, all Pearl Jam could do was gig and record material that made people think again. The buzz about the band was far outweighing the cynics, such that after only a handful of gigs talk turned to getting a record deal. At this point, Ament and Gossard's lengthy experience proved invaluable – Ament phoned up a contact of his at Epic, Michael Goldstone, who had enthusiastically signed up Mother Love Bone when he worked at PolyGram. Such was Ament's confidence that he dictated what the band would require in order to sign: 'It was exactly what we didn't do with Mother Love Bone,' Ament later told *Rip* magazine, 'and that was to actually get some of the spontaneity and freshness of the songs; to get really close to them when they were written. With Mother Love Bone, most of the songs on that record had been written for a year. That's the way a lot of music is made. It's an analytical process, where you try to write a certain kind of song for a certain kind of audience to sell a certain amount of product or records. I think that's not what it's about. I wanted to get back to making a record that was a little bit more raw, with a little more emphasis on getting the intensity.'

'When I first met him, there was something different about him. He was tremendously enigmatic and charismatic.' *Epic executive*

Eddie showed immediate signs of being far less comfortable with the business side than his band colleagues. In their opening meeting at Epic Records' offices, he spoke little and stared at his lap for most of the conversation. But an Epic executive who was in on these early discussions told *Rolling Stone*, 'When I first met him, there was something different about him. He was tremendously enigmatic and charismatic.' The naiveté he seemed to display was, of course, at complete odds with the wealth of knowledge he had gleaned from his days hustling on the San Diego club scene.

After submitting a demo tape and attending only a few meetings, Pearl Jam signed an eight-album deal with Epic. They immediately settled in to London Bridge Studios in Seattle with producer Rick Parashar to record their debut album for the major label. Pearl Jam were still less than five weeks old.

CHAPTER FOUR

ELEVEN INTO TEN MAKES 9 MILLION

'I'm much more happy in this band than any other band I've been in. It's just the way music should be.'

Jeff

The recording process for the debut album was as spontaneous and intense as the coming together of the band had been. Recording the tracks largely live, the sessions went quickly and were completed and mixed within eight weeks. Essentially the band saw the record as an excuse to put some material down so they could go out on tour. In stark contrast to the heavily-edited Mother Love Bone, Pearl Jam were loose. Song ideas, however basic, were recorded in their entirety, after which the band would collectively decide if the track was worth keeping. Gossard told *Rip* magazine, 'I feel like this band now is so much more open to new ideas and types of things. It's huge steps away from Mother Love Bone. In that sense, I think similar ideas that we would have had in Mother Love Bone that never came to fruition are actually being finished at this point. The more I play with Eddie, the more I hear how his vocals work, and the more he hears how I write songs, the better we'll get. I think that's what I am even more excited about. There are moments on the record that we have right now that aren't perfect, which is great. That's the kind of record we wanted to make.' A concrete example of this is 'Release'; it was created when Gossard was tuning up and the rest of the band joined in, and within twenty minutes the finished song was on tape.

Ament also sensed a new liberty in the studio: 'I'm much more happy in this band than any other band I've been in,' he stated. 'Everybody does their own thing. Nobody is telling anyone else that they're playing too much or too little. It just sort of falls into place. It's just the way music should be.' Eddie, in a fashion that was to become indicative of his complexity, was somewhat more obscure: 'When you're out in the desert,' he said in

Rolling Stone, 'you can't believe the amount of stars. We've sent mechanisms out there, and they haven't found anything. They've found different colours of sand, and rings and gases, but nobody's shown me anything that makes me feel secure in what happens afterward. All I really believe in is this fucking moment, like right now. And that, actually, is what the whole album talks about.'

After the recording, the tracks were mixed at Ridge Farm Studios in Dorking, England during May 1991, where the track listing was narrowed down to eleven. Taking its title from the number on Mookie Blaylock's basketball shirt, *Ten* was ready for release.

Ten was, on the surface, a rather depressing record. Eddie's lyrics spoke painfully of the homeless, incest, murder, suicide, depression, hospitalisation and insanity. However, there was something about the delivery, the dynamics between Gossard's thunderous rhythm guitar, McCready's fluttering lead and Eddie's baritone, screaming, yet delicate vocals that made the overall tone almost celebratory. Eddie seemed to switch with ease from ragged, gut-wrenching howls to booming croons. The thumping rhythm section made some of the songs instant rock anthems, and the music was generally uplifting, swirling through a myriad of moods.

'Everybody in the band was going through this kind of re-birth, and it went from the burdens of being alive to appreciating being alive.' *Eddie Vedder*

But it was Eddie's vocals and obscure yet incisive lyrics that made the record such an impressive start. He filled the album with ultra-real stories, riddles written to himself, people he had met or heard about, friends, relatives and enemies. Occasionally the music became dour trad-rock such as with the rather tiresome 'Porch', but this was the exception. Snatches of Led Zeppelin, Aerosmith, the Who, Neil Young, Kiss and various seventies rock acts could be heard breaking through the album, and McCready openly admitted that much of the record was a direct copy of Stevie Ray Vaughan, calling it 'a tribute rip off'.

Eddie refused to discuss his inspiration other than this small offering in *Rip*, where he said he drew his material from 'personal experience. It's all coming in from all these other sources . . . stuff that you see. Real life is so much more intense than any movie, any song, any book – if you join up and see the right performance. It's not something you could buy tickets for. Two nights ago I'm staying in the basement of this art gallery where we rehearse, and I was using the restroom at about three in the morning. I heard these drunks in the back alley. I went to listen through the crack in the door, because I thought I could hear them better. I could actually see through the half-inch clearing. It was more intense than any movie. It was all so real. There was a beginning, middle and end. It was like drugs, violence, all within less than twenty minutes. It was fascinating. If I could have actually sat in that alcove of the alley with them and had these three beers with them, I would have loved to. But then I wouldn't have seen what I saw . . .' (that experience became the song 'Even Flow'). This empathy with the disenchanted, the disillusioned and the disenfranchised was a characteristic of Eddie's from years ago, but with the higher profile that Pearl Jam's success was about to bring him, his feelings became public property.

Pearl Jam knew it was good: 'There are some moments on this record that are pretty incredible,' said Ament in *Rip*. 'At the same time, I think there's a real looseness about it. I think it properly captured where we were at as a band. I don't think it over-extended what we could do. I think it's a real honest record.' Eddie had this to say, 'Everybody in the band was going through this kind of re-birth, and it went from the burdens of being alive to appreciating being alive.'

Eddie Vedder has always said that he is not prepared to explain his lyrics, discuss them or pick them to pieces. When asked to do so in interviews, he flatly refuses or quickly changes the subject. On a couple of occasions, however, he has lowered his guard. One of these concerns the track that was the centre-piece of the debut album and a record that the *Los Angeles Times* crowned the 'My Generation' for Generation X – 'Alive'. The occasion of the discussion was an interview in *Rolling Stone* and it is quoted at length here: 'Everybody writes about it like it's a life-affirmation thing – I'm really glad about that. It's a great interpretation. But 'Alive' is . . . it's torture. Which is why it's fucked up for me.

Why I should probably learn how to sing another way. It would be easier. It's . . . it's too much.' Vedder continues: 'The story of the song is that a mother is with a father and the father dies. It's an intense thing because the son looks just like the father. The son grows up to be the father, the person that she lost. His father's dead, and now this confusion, his mother, his love, how does he love her, how does she love him? In fact, the mother, even though she marries somebody else, there's no one she's ever loved more than the father. You know how it is, first loves and stuff. And the guy dies. How could you ever get him back? But the son. He looks exactly like him. It's uncanny. So she wants him. The son

Eddie's performances were soon known for his stage diving.

is oblivious to it all. He doesn't know what the fuck is going on. He's still dealing, he's still growing up. He's still dealing with love, he's still dealing with the death of his father. All he knows is 'I'm still alive' – those three words, that's totally out of burden. But I'm still alive. I'm the lover that's still alive.'

The only setback in Pearl Jam's apparent rollercoaster ride was the departure of drummer Dave Krusen shortly after they finished mixing *Ten*. Krusen had always been a last-minute recruitment, and was maybe destined not to last the course. Although the departure was said to be amicable, the rumour-mongers inevitably whispered about drugs and drink, but the truth was rather less dramatic – he had been experiencing difficulties with his girlfriend and decided that domestic bliss should come before his career with Pearl Jam. A club tour was imminent, so it was far from a timely departure, forcing the band to scour for a new sticksman whilst New Bohemians' drummer Matt Chamberlain filled in during a three-week period in the late summer of 1991 (one of these gigs was recorded and used for a future video of 'Alive'). However, shortly after this club tour finished, Chamberlain was offered a slot on the *Saturday Night Live* show's resident band, which he felt offered him as lucrative and secure a position as he was ever likely to come across. On his way out, he recommended that Pearl Jam talk to a drummer he knew who played in a Dallas funk band called Dr Tongue and who co-hosted a radio show called *Music We Like* in Houston.

Dave Abbruzzese had always loved music, and from an early age played in ramshackle bands with generally tone-deaf friends. Born in Stanford, Connecticut in May 1968, his family had moved first to North Carolina and then settled in East Texas. Although he was the only member of his family interested in music, his parents did not discourage him. By his teens he was an avid drummer, nurturing an obsession that was such a focal point of his formative years that he dropped out of high school early so he could pursue music. 'Nothing else felt right to me, nothing else mattered,' he told *Modern Drummer* magazine. 'My theory at the time was that I could always go back to school, but I couldn't always seize the opportunities that were at my door then. Looking back, it was a huge gamble, and my Dad was right there wishing me the best, telling me that if I struck out, I was in for a hard life ahead of me. I had no sense of the gamble I was taking at the time. Ten years from now doesn't mean a thing; I may not even be around in ten years. The only thing that matters to me now is playing music, and I have to do it.'

It is worth remembering that at this stage, Pearl Jam's first record was yet to be released and they had no profile other than locally around Seattle. Subsequently, Abbruzzese was reluctant to commit himself to the band full-time. 'Pearl Jam had a record contract,' he recalls, 'but all that means is guaranteed debt. And they had a record I thought was cool, but that didn't guarantee any kind of success, either.' He enjoyed jamming with his friends Darrell Phillips and Pat Hooker in Dr Tongue, and he occasionally filled in for Matt Chamberlain if his friend couldn't fulfil a session slot he had booked or a gig he couldn't make. Also, Abbruzzese was uncomfortable with the musical direction Pearl Jam seemed to be aiming for: 'It seemed totally different from where I came from musically. I'd never heard Soundgarden or Mother Love Bone, or even knew anything about Seattle music. Where I came from was older music like Zeppelin and Sly And The Family Stone – stuff like that – all the way up to the Peppers. I was in more of a funky place, but my days were spent pretty much just hanging out with my buddies and playing music, not spending much time listening to new music.'

Abbruzzese met the band in his radio station's studio, where he played some of the tracks that later appeared on *Ten*. After that, he thought he had missed out, as he didn't hear from them for a few weeks, but then Eddie and Ament called up again and talked at length on the phone. They invited him to a gig for which Chamberlain was still filling in, after which they jammed as a whole band. Pearl Jam instantly liked him – Ament said, 'It was weird, we wanted to argue about it a little, but nobody really could.'

For Abbruzzese, however, there were some serious decisions to be had. He had a band in Dallas, a girlfriend, a big circle of friends and a life he enjoyed. After much thought, he made his move: 'All I ever thought about was playing music, so it didn't really catch me off guard. I just said "screw it" and went for it . . . I flew back to Texas, packed my stuff, patted my cat on the head, kissed my girlfriend goodbye, hopped in the truck, and drove to Seattle. We went on tour right after that.' Abbruzzese's initial reluctance dissipated with alarming speed – five days after joining the band, the new drummer had a tattoo cut into his shoulder of Ament's stick-man drawing that was used for the band's logo. He had only played two gigs.

Considering its subsequent success, *Ten* enjoyed a remarkably low profile on its release in autumn 1991. After a positive review in the *Tribune*, Eddie phoned up the journalist and talked for over an hour about his feelings about the record, and his expectations for

its success. He said he would be delighted if it could sell about 40,000 copies. He misjudged by about nine million. He also said he was looking forward to playing venues that could hold around 1000 people, calling them 'sacred places, churches of music'. On this too, his expectation was way out.

Initially, *Ten* only pierced the lower regions of the Billboard Top 200, but over the autumn, as the band worked hard promoting the record, it crept slowly upwards. Touring initially meant a series of club dates, driving round in a small, cramped van. To Abbruzzese's amazement, halfway through these gigs one of his favourite bands, the Red Hot Chili Peppers, asked Pearl Jam to support them on their *BloodSugarSexMagick* album tour. This fitted in nicely with a few headline slots of their own which included a date at the prestigious CBGB's in New York.

'But if you looked at his eyes, man, there was an intensity in what he was doing. That was his belief in himself.' *Jeff Ament*

Even at this early stage, the rest of the band realised that in Eddie Vedder they had stumbled across a compelling front man. He stalked around the stage, launching each vocal line with a growling, booming voice that belied his diminutive frame. He seemed to live each song, draining himself emotionally as he thrashed through the range of *Ten's* despairing characters. He often looked almost bemused as to where he was, and the mumbled comments that were barely audible in between songs added to this impression. Sometimes he rolled back his eyes into his skull and grimaced hard as he spat out his lyrics through clenched teeth; other times, his articulation was gentle, wide-eyed, almost child-like.

Apart from his baritone growl and introverted, intense stage persona, Eddie had a desire to climb around the stage that could verge on the suicidal. Ament remembered one particular occasion: 'I think the first time I got really worried, we were in Texas, and Eddie climbed up on this girder, about fifty feet in the air. Nobody knew where he was. And all of a sudden you look up – some guy had a flashlight on him – and it was like, "Fuck!" He's up there clinging to a girder, I'm thinking, "This guy is insane, but I'm so totally pumped."' Ament continued, 'That whole thing almost turned into a circus event. People weren't looking at his eyes when he was doing that. I think they were looking at the fucking freak, you know. The guy who was dumb enough to put his life on the line. Evel Knievel. But if you looked at his eyes, man, there was an intensity in what he was doing. That was his belief in himself. He was saying, "This isn't just 'rock' to me."' Eddie agreed, although he was soon to grow weary of his stage antics and jokingly told *Rolling Stone*: 'That climbing happened out of me saying, "Look, this is how extreme I feel about this situation. This is how fucking intense I'm taking this moment." You can't do that for long, because what they really want to see is, they want you to chop your fucking arm off, hold up your arm, wave it around spewing blood, and believe me, if you did that, the crowd would go fucking ballistic. You only get four good shows like that, though. Four good shows, and then you're just a torso and a head, trying to get one of your band mates to give you one last hurrah and chop your head off. Which they probably wouldn't do, which would really be hell. But they'd say, "Sing from your diaphragm, at least you still have that going for you!"'

Onstage, the rest of the band were hardly static either. Pearl Jam seemed to possess the ability to walk on stage and hit peak intensity within 30 seconds of the opening song. Their early gigs were aleady tumultuous, almost violent affairs – Abbruzzese thrashed away at his kit, hair and sticks blurring together in such a frenzy that he frequently could not flex his hands afterwards due to the scores of thick blisters. Ament was Viking-like, thumping around the stage on his bass guitar, which was scratched with the names of his favourite basketball players and teams. Behind him, his enormous bass speaker stacks pounded out the rhythm, where small plastic models of those same sportsmen quivered from the vibrations. Gossard and McCready seemed to want to break their guitar strings, such was the venom with which they attacked each song, and the chemistry between the two was clearly at the very core of Pearl Jam's live strength. This powerful live show played a key part in building Pearl Jam's massive success, but despite the other members' ability, Eddie was the star attraction from the outset.

By Christmas, the Pearl Jam rollercoaster was really starting to gain momentum. Record sales were high and their gigs were sold out. On the final day of the year, the band took part in a concert that was to become legendary. The New Year's Eve show at San Francisco's Cow Palace had an awesome bill – Pearl Jam, Nirvana and headliners the Red Hot Chili Peppers. Normally, the city that had brought us Flower Power was dominated on the last night of the year by the Grateful Dead's annual show at the Oakland Coliseum, with hippy clothes and sweet smelling fumes once more swamping the area. However, this year, in the middle of this loved-up time warp came thousands of long-haired losers streaming down from Seattle, complete with grunge music, skateboards, ripped jeans and combat boots.

'I don't take it for granted to be able to express myself in music, so to be given a stage to do it from, that's an awesome responsibility.' *Eddie Vedder*

Over 16,000 of them jammed into the Cow Palace for a concert that in many ways was a celebration of the triumph of rock's new generation. The anachronistic hippies amassing round the corner were spared little abuse, as each of the three bands sarcastically dissed them. Pearl Jam opened, and Eddie walked on stage, smiling broadly for once, and said provocatively, 'Want to hear some songs by the Dead?' His fans booed loudly and the set blasted off with a powerful a cappella version of Fugazi's anti-rape song 'Suggestion'. Eddie finished it with the warning, 'Don't go partying on other people's pussies unless they want you to,' a thinly-veiled reference to the Red Hot Chili Peppers yob anthem 'Party On Your Pussy'. He ended the set by clambering up the lighting rig and plunging into the swarming masses below.

For once, however, the night was not Eddie's. In the wake of the enormous success of *Nevermind* (it had reached Number 1 in the Billboard charts that very week) and the swift canonisation of Kurt Cobain, the stars were always going to be Nirvana. Their guitar-smashing and ear-splitting set was also the most powerful, and made life somewhat difficult for the Chili Peppers to close the evening. However, Eddie Vedder still managed to grab some limelight by being the final stage diver of the night during a rousing encore of 'Yertle The Turtle'. Anyone who was there left the building knowing that they were unlikely to see a concert like it again.

Pearl Jam kicked off 1992 as they meant to carry on – touring – and with Eddie in seemingly optimistic spirits, telling the *Tribune*: 'I don't take it for granted to be able to express myself in music, so to be given a stage to do it from, that's an awesome responsibility.' After some brief dates in Scandinavia, they headed for England, where they started off in the rather lugubrious surroundings of the lager lout capital of the Southeast, Southend. In typically pretentious fashion, London demanded a showcase gig for the media and industry, a 'secret' show that only industry insiders would be able to get tickets for. When Pearl Jam arrived at the Borderline for it, they were appalled to see hundreds of fans waiting hopelessly outside for tickets they could never buy. The band spent the time they should have been doing soundchecks by chatting to these fans and handing out free CDs, so as to atone for the privileges of the media types inside.

The five that made Ten *– the original line-up with drummer Dave Kreusen (middle).*

CHAPTER FIVE

ABUSE

*'I do feel a duty to warn the kids about false music that's
claiming to be underground or alternative. They're just jumping
on the alternative bandwagon.'*

Kurt Cobain

In a way to which Pearl Jam would become accustomed,
their growing success drew as much criticism as it did
praise. What was so stinging about the first major public
volley of abuse was that it came from fellow musicians – from
Nirvana, or more specifically Kurt Cobain. As sales of *Ten*
accelerated, caught up with and then passed the already massive
sales of *Nevermind*, Cobain became increasingly vocal about his
dislike of Eddie's band. In a series of scathing attacks in *Rolling
Stone* and *Musician* magazine, he gave vent to his doubts about
them: 'I know for a fact that at the very least, if not Stoney, then
Jeff is a definite careerist – a person who will kiss ass to make sure
his band gets popular so he can become rich.' Kurt also claimed
that Pearl Jam were 'responsible for this corporate, alternative,
cock-rock fusion' and he later said, with regard to the continuing
comparisons between the two groups, 'I would love to be erased
from my association with that band.' When asked why he was
being so vindictive, he said, 'I do feel a duty to warn the kids about
false music that's claiming to be underground or alternative.
They're just jumping on the alternative bandwagon.' In Cobain's
eyes, Pearl Jam and Eddie Vedder just did not mean what they said
– the clothes and haircuts fitted, but the music and ethics didn't.

Cobain was not alone in his reservations. Pearl Jam's
detractors looked at Eddie Vedder as a Jim Morrisson clone, the
packaged rock star with his apparently difficult childhood, his
overtly pained stage persona and grumbling offstage principles.
They looked to the fact that Pearl Jam signed with a major label
within weeks of forming, via one of the band's corporate friends,
and questioned their underground integrity, especially the massive
amounts of money Epic spent creating a following that genuine

bands had to garner through hard work. They looked to the band's heritage, and the careerist background of Green River and Mother Love Bone, especially quoting Mark Arm's reasons for splitting from Green River because Ament and Gossard were too calculating about their drive to succeed, and Arm's horror when Ament declared he was determined to be 'a professional musician'. They looked at the MTV saturation of the 'Alive' video and the 'fake' radio-friendly rock the band produced that was swamping the airwaves. They cited the band's apparently inoffensive appeal, pleasing both youngsters wrapped up in the grunge/Seattle phenomenon and their fathers, trading on their seventies rock roots. Pearl Jam became the purists' scapegoats for all that was wrong with Seattle and grunge, in particular the incipient corporate hijack of the scene. Cobain's remarks spearheaded the accusations.

'I'm not up there playing to get women. I'm not up there playing to get money. I'm not interested in that.' *Eddie Vedder*

The band themselves were taken aback by the ferocity of these attacks. They had publicly declared their respect, and indeed debt, to Nirvana, and had never bad-mouthed Cobain. Plus, there were very real examples of why these criticisms were not justified. Eddie would later personally instigate a whole host of uncommercial edicts for the band – secret shows for fan club members only, the release of vinyl two weeks before the CD, moderate ticket prices and cheap merchandise, live concert broadcasts, and so on. Later Pearl Jam went on to stop making videos or giving press interviews. In the immediate short-term, the band simply took Cobain's 'cock rock' accusations and slapped it on the back of their own T-shirt.

Eddie was mortified by the attacks and he felt drawn to defend himself: 'If people are gonna pay some attention,' he told *Downtown Edition*, 'I just better make sure that what I'm saying has text and means something – and is true to myself and true to music. I'm not a fucking poser, and I'll fight for that.

That's something I take seriously. I'm not up there playing to get women. I'm not up there playing to get money. I'm not interested in that. So what am I doing? I'm playing for music.' He also said, 'So can you be famous and alternative at the same time? That's the question. If they say that after they've seen the show, then I might be a little bummed out. The fact is our music comes from a totally honest place. I think Kurt is concerned, as I am, that the image of Seattle – whatever the fuck that is – will be more rock than punk. I personally don't want to be involved in the rock side if that's what he thinks.'

In retrospect, the accusations appear hypocritical. There appeared to be no record of Nirvana wailing and screaming when they signed to Geffen, one of the world's biggest record companies. If Pearl Jam were merely regurgitating seventies rock, then Nirvana could reasonably be accused of just resurrecting seventies hard rock like Black Sabbath and Deep Purple. There was a contradiction in that Pearl Jam were accused on the one hand of being overnight sensations, while on the other they were ridiculed for having as individuals a lengthy past trying to make it on the underground. How could Green River be an extrusion of corporate vileness when they were universally acknowledged as having been a key, if not the central, agent for the entire Sub Pop/Seattle scene? Also, Nirvana's *Nevermind* received similarly huge amounts of promotion, both from their record company, and from MTV, who played the 'Smells Like Teen Spirit' video as much as any other that year. Indeed, whereas Nirvana had recorded their video specifically for MTV use, Pearl Jam had recorded a live video because they were told MTV would not play this format very often. Also, Cobain had never at this point met or talked to Eddie. It all smacked of bitterness.

To be fair to Cobain, there was an element at work of the press blowing the rivalry out of all proportion for the sake of good copy. To his credit, Cobain later retracted much of what he had said: 'I'm not going to do that anymore, it hurts Eddie and he's a good guy.' He also said, 'I later found out that Eddie basically found himself in this position. He never claimed to be anybody who supports any kind of punk ideals in the first place.' Conversely, and rather ironically, Pearl Jam later started to agree with some of Cobain's concerns, telling *Musician* magazine, 'All the things Kurt Cobain said we were guilty of, we were – on some level. Kurt had us pegged in a lot of ways. Somebody from the outside can sometimes see the ugliness in our situation more clearly. He saw us in a way that was accurate to him. I can only say that I don't want . . . I don't think that I'm exclusively what he, at one point, claimed we were! Which was everything bad about rock music in terms of the music not coming first. Jeff and I have been very driven about wanting to be successful – sometimes at the expense of a lot of people's feelings – without even realising it. Our wanting to get things done has ruffled a lot of feathers and stepped on a few toes.'

'Jeff and I have been very driven about wanting to be successful – sometimes at the expense of a lot of people's feelings – without even realising it.' *Eddie Vedder*

The rivalry was well and truly laid to rest at an MTV Awards ceremony. Eddie had been slow-dancing with Courtney Love to Eric Clapton's 'Tears In Heaven' when Cobain suddenly butted in and started dancing with him: 'I stared into his eyes and told him that I thought he was a respectable human,' Kurt said. 'And I did tell him straight out that I still think his band sucks. I said, "After watching you perform, I realised that you are a person that does have some passion." It's not a fully contrived thing. There are plenty of other more evil people out in the world than him and he doesn't deserve to be scapegoated like that.' For his part, Eddie was happy to let the whole confrontation die: 'There was a lot of stuff that got said, but none of it really matters,' he told *Melody Maker*. 'And I like to think he may have had second thoughts about some of the things he said, you know. Because so much bullshit was getting written about us. I remember going out surfing the next morning and remembering how good that moment felt and thinking, "Fuck, man, if only we hadn't been so afraid of each other." Because we were going though so much of the same shit. If only we'd talked, maybe we could have helped each other . . .'

Eddie in New York, with his treasured yellow 'lyric' suitcase that he took everywhere.

Eddie Vedder had seemed reasonably well equipped to deal with his new found fame. However, he was soon to learn that the rough had to be taken with the smooth.

The first problems came in the UK, in Manchester, where the band enjoyed their gig and chatted with local fans backstage – Pearl Jam are noted for their decidedly low-key behind-the-scenes habits, with a distinct absence of drugs, supermodels and general debauchery. Everyone enjoyed a great night, but when they headed outside they found that their tour van had been robbed, while their tour manager had been held at knife-point. Local kids had broken the locks and humped the gear over a nearby wall. Disgusted and feeling let down, Pearl Jam wearily climbed into the damaged van for the journey to their next gig. They chose not to report the matter to the police.

After more UK dates the band flew back home for a brief respite, only to find that *Ten* was selling so solidly that everyone wanted an interview. In the UK the 'Alive' single had reached the Top Twenty and across Europe the reception was similar – the stakes were rising all the time. At home, the band received their first industry recognition of this success when the Northwest Music Awards voted them Best Rock Album, Best New Group and Best Electric Guitar (for McCready). Such was Pearl Jam's high profile now that they were invited on to the enormously popular *Saturday Night Live* show. Eddie found himself uneasy with these accolades – when they later played *The Late Show With David Letterman* he phoned the host ahead of their appearance and personally asked him not to over-promote their performance. On air, Eddie was unable to resist *Saturday Night Live's* multi-million audience and pulled his T-shirt towards the camera to reveal the words 'No Bush 92' in reference to the forthcoming election campaign (which Bush lost). The camera swiftly jumped away from the offending garment on to the drum kit, which was just as well, because Eddie's T shirt also carried a drawing of a coat-hanger, an image used by the Pro Choice movement to remind people that it was the instrument of choice for backstreet abortions.

The television industry's recognition of the band went one further in May 1992, when Pearl Jam were asked to play an acoustic set for the highly popular *MTV Unplugged* series of concerts. Already a long list of rock luminaries had performed these sets for the music channel, and with the release of hugely successful tie-in CDs soon after, many acts such as Led Zeppelin, the Cure and Nirvana were to enjoy enormous commercial benefits from their appearances on this show.

This was not the first time Pearl Jam had performed such a gig – during their recent European tour they had endured a terrible evening in Milan where the 200-capacity club had sold over 500 tickets, the sound system was diabolical and the whole event a catastrophe. Three days later they drove to a show in Zurich, where they arrived to find the club was even smaller and apparently even more poorly equipped. Faced with another night of fighting against the odds, the band decided instead to play acoustically, encouraged in no small part by the fact the stage was too small for a drum kit! They hired three acoustic guitars, a kick drum and a bongo, and took the chance. It was to turn out to be one of their finest shows to date.

Some detractors were confident that the band, with some of the cock-rock accusations still ringing in their ears, would be unable to pull off the rather more subtle and controlled task of playing in these intimate and minimalist surroundings. Events did not help, when the equipment Pearl Jam had ordered did not turn up and at the last minute they were forced to use inferior, borrowed instruments. Ament did not get a bass and McCready's acoustic was too badly constructed to play any lead solos. A late night phonecall to some friends at least managed to secure them a couple of guitars that they were more comfortable with.

Eddie sat on a simple stool throughout most of the show, and his baritone growls seemed to shift a pitch, sounding less violent but with the same anguish and passion. Perhaps the highlight was at the end of 'Black' when he poured his heart out, at which point he seemed to be totally exposed. For the rest of the band it was a real challenge. 'It was weird,' McCready told *Guitar World*, 'because it forces you to play differently, you can't rely on feedback. It forces you to use dynamics, and to look at each song in a different way. Some songs turned out good acoustically, and some just didn't quite happen.' Gossard obviously enjoyed it much more: 'An acoustic show is really sort of a naked, exposed way of playing your songs, because you can't hide behind distortion. Doing it in front of millions of people is even more intimidating. We actually went out there and had a fun, energised show. It's a cool way to hear the band, because the drums and the vocals are featured a lot more . . . Eddie can really shine when he's given room to move around vocally. It gave people a different perception of the band.'

Commercially, as Gossard pointed out, it was an excellent opportunity for Pearl Jam to showcase a side of their talents that much of the public thought did not exist. In the process, this reinforced their rapidly growing status, and after *Unplugged* their fan club membership doubled. On a more worrying note, letters addressed personally to Eddie became more and more intense: 'I was recently considering suicide, and then I heard your music . . .'

Such was the growing success of Pearl Jam that they were in a position to arrange a free concert in the Seattle Gas Works Park on the Saturday preceding Memorial Day in late May 1992, in support of the 'Rock The Vote' cause. Applications were made for permits and arrangements began to take shape at this communal park on the edge of the city, including a massive stage, and a 15-foot-high skateboard ramp for use by some of the top local skaters. The idea had originally been mooted before Pearl Jam set off on their European and American tour to promote *Ten*. That was also before they were catapulted into the higher echelons of the Billboard charts, before they started to compete with Nirvana as the biggest alternative band in the world and before *Ten* had gone multi-platinum. Back then, the band thought a free concert on their triumphant return was a fitting thank-you to their local fans, which would probably attract maybe somewhere in the region of 5000 kids. In the ensuing period, which incredibly was only just over three months, their popularity had grown so massively that attendance figures in the region of 30,000 were now being discussed. Unfortunately, this was just too much for the old conservative heads on the council, especially Seattle's mayor, Norm Rice. Concern was voiced about support bands, punk rockers Seaweed and Seven Year Bitch, and grave suspicions about the skateboard fraternity were also raised. Three days before the celebratory concert was scheduled to take place, the city's parks department refused the permit to perform. So much for encouraging young people to vote. Not for the first or last time Eddie was seething in the face of bureaucratic idiocy.

He was livid for a number of reasons. For one, the city's parks department had no objections to a crowd of around 40,000 turning up for the fireworks party to celebrate Memorial Day the following weekend. Eddie told *Melody Maker* he felt the recent Los Angeles riots may have been a misinformed factor in the mayor's objection: 'You know, a lot of work was put into it, we knew what we were doing. We knew we could easily deal with however many people turned up, but the Mayor and his people didn't agree. But it wasn't the *number* of people that bothered them, it was the *type* of people – 30,000 *young* people, 30,000 *alternative* people. They couldn't have been worried about riots, because this was gonna be a coming together of people for a positive reason. If anything, it would've overshadowed the riots. There was nothing negative about it . . .'

'But it wasn't the number of people that bothered them, it was the type of people – 30,000 young people, 30,000 alternative people.' *Eddie Vedder*

He also hated the fact that it was such a late cancellation – hundreds of kids had already driven in packed little vans towards the Seattle park, and some local TV crews had filmed their arrival. There were even reports that a plane had been chartered to bring 2000 kids from Alaska. Eddie was further angered by his personal failure to bring about something he had wanted to achieve. This last point is indicative of his intense drive – he loves to overcome obstacles, beat difficulties, and challenge himself with increasingly difficult opponents. With the Gasworks Park show cancelled, his frustration at being denied a permit was equalled by his exasperation at not being able to do anything about it.

In the wake of the cancellation, Eddie couldn't just let things pass. In the immediate term, he drove to the park on the day of the concert, and to the amazement of the dozens of kids who had arrived, chatted to them, signed autographs and apologised personally for having wasted their time. He also decided to have the skateboard ramp built anyway, entirely at his own expense, on a piece of private land out of the jurisdiction of the mayor. When *Melody Maker* arrived to check the site out they were impressed: 'It is amazing. The ramp, almost complete, stands in the middle of an emerald-green clearing in a thick forest. All over it and around it are the skaters – tall, bronzed demi-gods, bare-chested in psychedelic Paisley shorts.' Eddie told the reporter, 'Skaters have this weird cosmic energy, when they're catching air flying off the top of the ramp, it's like when you surf, when you feel the power of the ocean, the rhythm of the waves.' Standing there doing the interview, watching the kids skate and talk and be free of constraints, Eddie was smiling once again, his seething resentment having ebbed away in the face of positive action: 'The people who wind up with their foot in their mouth are the people who don't mean it, don't live it. I live this stuff. I did it before the band, and I'll do it after. This is my life . . .'

In the longer term, Eddie re-arranged the gig for a time and place when he could guarantee the permits would be issued. Hordes of angry phonecalls, letters and faxes denouncing the myopia of the authorities had followed the cancellation. In response, a re-scheduling was offered for the next Wednesday, but Eddie turned this down as it was on a school day. Finally, in September 1992, a show did take place, re-located to Magnusson Park. Over 29,000 free tickets were put on offer at 8am on a Saturday morning, and within twenty minutes the roads were blocked within a two-mile radius of the ticket centre. Pearl Jam picked up the entire $100,000 bill for the concert, including an extensive free bus service. The gig was warmly received, and the band enjoyed finally having their own way, especially Eddie. The only downside for him were some of the comments fans made to him about his delayed victory against the authorities. They said he was fighting for them, representing them, leading them even. He shifted uneasily at these words, telling *Melody Maker,* 'That's the trouble with all this. It's putting me into a position I'm very uncomfortable with. It's making me like a spokesperson or something.'

Without pause for breath, Pearl Jam flew back to Europe for yet more dates, starting off with a support slot in 'The Cult In The Park' show in London's Finsbury Park, where they also played alongside the late-lamented Ned's Atomic Dustbin and the godfathers of British indie guitar music, Mega City Four. Then it was back to the continent, where events started to turn sour, and Eddie hit a brick wall.

The problems arose in Stockholm. The gig was packed and the band were in high spirits. They played brilliantly, and because the crowd responded so warmly, they extended their set and enjoyed over two hours of music, genuine rapport and friendship with their fans. Then, in an echo of their Manchester experience, when they went backstage, they found their dressing room had been broken into and lots of personal belongings stolen, including Eddie's precious lyric book and journals, taken from inside the precious yellow tweed suitcase that he took with him everywhere.

Pearl Jam on MTV Unplugged *in May 1992, with Dave Abbruzzese by now a familiar figure on drums.*

Although Eddie had suggested he might give these notes away at the end of the tour (he had previously given away a backpack with hand-written accounts of each show on tour), the theft devastated him. After such a great show, Eddie felt his trust with the crowd had been utterly broken. He hardly spoke that night.

The following day, the band were booked to play the Roskilde Festival outside Copenhagen in front of 70,000 people, and it took some persuading to even get Eddie on stage. He was so depressed and in such a dark mood that the performance was a disaster. The crowds were unruly anyway, as Denmark were playing Italy in a World Cup soccer match, and the rowdy throngs were swelled by drunken football yobs. At one point during 'Deep', Eddie ventured into the crowd, as he usually does, and disappeared, much to the band's concern as they knew what a foul frame of mind he was in. However, when he came to clamber back, the security didn't recognise him and refused to let him jump back on stage, thinking he was just another stage-diver. When Eddie became aggressive and loud they started punching him. McCready and Abbruzzese immediately jumped down and started fighting with the security, as did the band's tour manager, and in the middle of the mêlée Eddie was being heavily beaten. The mood backstage afterwards was appalling – Eddie was now palpably distressed and inconsolably low. After a brief discussion, they cancelled the remainder of their tour, giving the official reason as Eddie having 'exhaustion', saying he needed to rest.

> **'I feel like I ended up giving so much of myself away that I lost touch with what I was doing and why I was doing it.'** *Dave Abbruzzese*

They flew home the next day. On landing at the airport, Eddie, who had hardly spoken now for two days, was informed that a close friend, Stephanie Sargent, from the punk band Seven Year Bitch, had just died from an overdose. He was distraught. The meteoric rise and at times bizarre events of the last year seemed to catch up with him all at once, leaving him emotionally shattered. Rumours had it that his friends feared for his mental health.

Shortly after returning home, Eddie was sitting alone on a coastal sand bank, thinking about his recent life and the loss of Sargent. Suddenly, from behind him he heard young voices singing the Pearl Jam track 'Black', which for Eddie had become the perfect summary of the over-commercialisation of his band. He was so embroiled in his despair at this point that he got up, walked over to the speechless crowd of hikers and asked them to please stop singing his song.

Eddie was not alone in being distressed. The whole band were reeling from their rapid rise to fame, Abbruzzese expressed the effect this had had on his own personal life to *Modern Drummer*

Dave Grohl, Kurt Cobain and Krist Novoselic.

magazine: 'It really took its toll on us individually. For me, it just left me with a sense of feeling shattered . . . I feel like I ended up giving so much of myself away that I lost touch with what I was doing and why I was doing it. I basically lost a grip on what I was all about, and I didn't start being aware of how I felt and come to grips with the whole thing until we got off tour and went back home. I didn't go back to Texas, though; I stayed in Seattle because I felt like I needed to be alone. Over a year's time had passed, and my whole life was completely different. My relationship had taken a permanent sabbatical, and I had pretty much cut myself off from a lot of people who still mean a lot to me.' In the event, the band had little time to recuperate, as they were due to head back out on the road in just three weeks.

CHAPTER SIX

UP WITH THE STARS

'If it wasn't for music, I would have shot myself in front of that classroom.'

Eddie

Pearl Jam's invitation to join Lollapalooza was to catapult them on to an even higher level of success. Lollapalooza was designed as a travelling amalgam of cool music and topical issues and in many ways was the perfect vehicle for Eddie Vedder to reach more people. The brain-child of Perry Farrell, frontman for the defunct Jane's Addiction, was a touring package intended to showcase a myriad of musical styles while offering information about a variety of important political issues, thus creating an enjoyable and educated environment and forum for debate. At each of the 34 stadium-sized shows there would be stalls organised by major and minor protest groups, such as Greenpeace, gun control lobbyists and civil liberties groups. Stalls representing Rock The Vote stood next to People For The Ethical Treatment Of Animals, and Pro-Choice Lobbyists pitched near to Pro-Life campaigners. Tattooists and fire-eaters (Jim Rose's Circus Sideshow became enormously popular during this tour) added to the general Bohemian atmosphere. On the music side, Lush, Pearl Jam, Jesus and Mary Chain, Soundgarden, Ice Cube, Ministry, and the Red Hot Chili Peppers performed on the main stage, while a side stage offered less well-known acts the chance to break through.

It was a recession-beating package, and Eddie should have been in his element. With *Ten* nestling strongly in the Top 5, Pearl Jam were the highest-placed chart act on the bill, and the fervour which usually met them on their 3pm, second-on-the-bill-of-seven slot, reflected this. Even so, Eddie seemed far from relaxed. At a show at the Blossom Music Center, where torrential rain had turned the grounds into a quagmire, he sprang on to the stage screaming at the 20,000 crowd, 'I dare them to ignore me! I dare them to ignore me!' Understandably, nobody did. With the diversity of music on offer, and a marathon twelve hours per show, this was the real Woodstock for the nineties generation, not the bloated, corporate affair in New York state. Eddie closed the set at one show by telling the bemused security guards, who were vainly trying to control the seething mosh pit, 'We're redistributing the wealth.' However, it was rumoured that backstage Eddie was not enjoying himself . . .

'Some songs just aren't meant to be played between Hit Number 2 and Hit Number 3.' *Eddie Vedder*

While the band had been on the road, *Ten* had been selling massively. Eventually, the album passed the five million mark, and stayed on the *Billboard* charts for over 100 weeks. Its slow growth had turned into genuine longevity. Only Billy Ray Cirus's country album *Some Gave All* had kept the record off the Number 1 slot at the album's peak in August. In reality, while the band had been on the road, they had been catapulted from a moderately popular alternative band to one of the biggest acts in the world, and by definition Eddie now had one of the highest profiles in rock. Despite the lengthy careers of most of Pearl Jam's members, this phenomenal explosion still felt like an overnight sensation, and the massive personal and professional repercussions this huge demand would have on the respective members would have far-reaching effects. But at this early stage, Eddie was still enamoured by the success: 'In the old days, it was a dream to maybe not have to work the midnight shift, and somehow pay your rent by getting a cheque for your art. And, believe me, the first cheque I got from a publishing company was an emotional moment for me, because it was given to me for something that came out of my head.'

In September 1992, when sales might have been slowing down, the European release of the single 'Jeremy' propelled the album on to even greater success. Eddie had long since registered his aversion to singles, particularly with songs that were so emotionally complex: 'Some songs,' he told *Rolling Stone*, 'just aren't meant to be played between Hit Number 2 and Hit

With the release of 'Jeremy', Pearl Jam's popularity soared.

Number 3. You start doing those things, you'll crush it. That's not why we wrote songs. We didn't write to make hits. But those fragile songs get crushed by the business. I don't want to be a part of it. I don't think the band wants to be part of it.' Even so, under pressure from Epic, 'Jeremy' had been released. It was a massive hit and won Pearl Jam several MTV Awards (at the ceremony a thoroughly miserable Eddie told the 50 million viewers, alluding to the song's theme, 'If it wasn't for music, I would have shot myself in front of that classroom.').

Stone and Jeff let loose at a Lollapalooza gig.

As with so many of Eddie's lyrics, the inspiration behind 'Jeremy' was a real-life tragedy. In this case, a sixteen-year-old sophomore, Jeremy Wade Delle, described as a loner, put a .357-calibre Magnum into his mouth at 9.45am and shot himself dead, in front of a class of schoolmates. The incident occurred at Richardson High School in Texas, where Jeremy, who had been receiving counselling, had recently been transferred from Dallas.

He had missed class the day before, and his teacher had asked him to collect an admission slip from the secretary's office (his attendance had been increasingly erratic, and his divorced father had even been called to the school). Jeremy left the classroom, but instead of doing as his teacher requested, he returned with the gun, walked directly to the front of the class and said, 'Miss, I got what I really went for,' then shot himself in the head. The suicide happened so swiftly no-one could stop it. The teacher stood against the wall crying and shaking, with some children supporting her. A note given by Jeremy to a classmate turned out to be a suicide letter. One classmate told a local paper, 'He was real quiet and he acted down at times. He acted sad.' One friend he talked to was sixteen-year-old Lisa Moore who would pass notes back and forth to him during class. She told police he usually signed his missives 'Write back' but just before the suicide had been ending them with the words 'Later days'.

'The first cheque I got from a publishing company was an emotional moment for me, because it was given to me for something that came out of my head.' *Eddie Vedder*

Eddie was deeply moved by this tragedy, and the song reflects his feelings. However, canonisation of the young man was not his intention. He was quite clear, at this point, about the pointlessness of taking one's own life: 'You kill yourself and you make a big old sacrifice and try to get your revenge. That all you're gonna end up with is a paragraph in a newspaper. Sixty-three degrees and cloudy in a suburban neighbourhood . . . in the end, it does nothing . . . nothing changes. The world goes on and you're gone. The best revenge is to live on and prove yourself. Be stronger than those people.'

Eddie himself saw this edict as central to his own life; he was determined to come back stronger against all his detractors, rather than caving in. Ironically, it was this tale of an emotionally broken youth that was one of the key factors in Eddie's own escalating success. MTV picked up on the story-based video, and immediately placed it on their so-called 'heavy rotation' schedule, guaranteeing it several plays a day for weeks. Eddie was incensed, feeling that this endless exposure on television sterilised what he had intended to be a powerful and poignant song.

Partially as a result of the over-use of the 'Jeremy' promo, the band decided to stop making videos altogether. Eddie hated the medium, and he was not alone. Jeff Ament recalled one incident in *Rolling Stone* when Mark Eitzel from American Music Club had jammed with him one night and then said, 'I liked your hit but the video sucked. It ruined my vision of the song.' Ament told the rest of the band and they never forgot those words. 'Ten years from now, I don't want people to remember our songs as videos,' says Ament.

'The best revenge is to live on and prove yourself. Be stronger than those people.' *Eddie Vedder*

Largely due to this massive international coverage, 'Jeremy' reached the Top Ten in both the USA and UK. Its success was controversial, with some parents blaming Pearl Jam for inspiring acts of violence, such as one kid who held his schoolfriends hostage. Understandably, the band utterly rejected these accusations (they didn't even know this had occurred until a radio phone-in fan told them live on air).

Pearl Jam rounded off 1992 with a spate of odd celebrity concerts. First up was the thirtieth anniversary gig for Bob Dylan at Madison Square Garden in New York. They found themselves alongside such pop luminaries as Lou Reed, Stevie Wonder, Eric Clapton and Tom Petty, and enjoyed blasting out Dylan's 'Masters Of War' as a one-off tribute. Next up came Neil Young's sixth annual Bridge Street Benefit in Mountain View, California, where Eddie played alongside names such as Elton John, Sammy Hagar and James Taylor. Then on New Year's Eve, they supported Keith Richards' solo band, the Xpensive Winos, at a secret New York gig (Pearl Jam later turned down a support slot on the Rolling Stones' next world tour). Then, with 1993 barely begun, Eddie performed with the re-united members of the Doors for a brief three-song set to herald their induction into Rock And Roll's Hall Of Fame. Further comparisons were made between Eddie and the late Jim Morrison, but the Pearl Jam frontman was coy about such compliments: 'My voice has just got the right register, it fits right in – that's why they chose me.' With a later appearance at Roger Daltrey's fiftieth Birthday celebration concert in New York's Carnegie Hall, some eyebrows were raised at the way Pearl Jam were mixing with the elite establishment rockers, but the band didn't care – they were in this for a good time, after a successful but fraught year. They saw the New Year in by getting blind drunk with Keith Richards, one of rock 'n' roll's greatest animals.

Backstage at a Lollapalooza gig in 1992 with the Pearl Jam crew.

CHAPTER SEVEN

FIVE BUYERS A SECOND

'Just being able to see Neil Young every night from the front of the stage was amazing, I've never seen better – so tight, but laid-back and groovy too.'

Stone

For the recording of the follow-up to *Ten*, Pearl Jam moved to the Site, a plush recording facility in the green hills outside San Francisco. Many big names had previously used this studio, and a lot of blockbuster film soundtracks had also been recorded there. Its idyllic surroundings were in the middle of one of the Bay area's most expensive real estate zones, where the studio managers who show visitors around the plot say, 'George Lucas owns everything to the left.' Private and luxurious, it should have been the ideal environment for Pearl Jam to record an unhurried and focussed second album when they arrived in February.

Of course, with Eddie in the band, things were never that simple. The start was good. With new producer, Atlanta-born Brendan O'Brien, at the helm, the recording process was substantially more fluid than it had been on *Ten*. O'Brien had a string of high-profile mixing and engineering credits to his name, including the Black Crowes, Dan Baird, and the Pearl Jam-influenced Stone Temple Pilots, as well as their old friends the Red Hot Chili Peppers' multi-platinum *BloodSugarSexMagick*. O'Brien had actually worked with the band before, producing their fan-club-only Christmas single 'Sonic Reducer', a cover of the excellent Dead Boys original. Himself a blues guitar player of some repute (he had played acclaimed lead guitar on Mick Jagger's 'Wandering Spirit'), O'Brien intuitively understood the musicians' needs and his almost-live approach to recording seemed to suit the band perfectly. Rather than record each part individually and build up the song as a composite, O'Brien preferred to mic the entire band up simultaneously and aim for first takes on everything. The result, when it worked, was spontaneous and vibrant.

All was going extremely well for the first week, with several tracks completed in rich bursts of inspiration. Already they had 'Rats', 'Go', 'Blood' and a slower version of their live staple 'Leash'. Then things started to go stale and the live process seemed to be running down. The rest of the band avoided getting tense and tried to step back and relax. Eddie, however, cleared off. He couldn't handle the environment and felt the plush surroundings were stifling his creativity. He told *Rolling Stone* about his exasperation: 'I fucking hate it here, I've had a hard time. How do you make a rock record here? Maybe the old rockers, maybe they love this. Maybe they need the comfort and the relaxation. Maybe they need it to make dinner music.' Eddie vanished into the depths of San Francisco for several days, failing to tell the rest of the band where he was. He drove round the city and even hiked in the wooded hills around the Bay's outskirts, getting a rash from poison ivy in the process. He needed to dwell on the songs, be alone with his thoughts and away from the studio. The band had written a lot of music and Eddie was flagging behind with his lyrics. His revulsion against the studio conditions exacerbated his mental block and he found the intensity just too much. However, the solitary break worked, although it did little to calm the rest of the band's nerves.

'You could tell when the music wanted to change just by the way he was singing.' *Stone Gossard*

On his return, Eddie seemed brighter and more at ease, and thereafter the recording process progressed unhindered. Within eight weeks the album was finished. Part of the reason for this swift completion was O'Brien's loose approach, but also Eddie was in on the music from the start for the first time and could really make an input. Whereas with *Ten* he had simply responded to some demo recordings, here he was part of the record's creation. A good example of that is 'w.m.a.'. The Seattle rehearsal studio they used before the actual recording was next to some fairly seedy streets where homeless people mixed with drug addicts and down-trodden immigrants, all of whom were seen as fair game to the local police force. One evening on his way back from the grocery store, Eddie watched in horror as several homeless men got some pretty rough treatment from the police. He returned to the studio enraged and pent up. The band were working on a loose arrangement they had written some time ago, which was largely drum and bass, and Eddie just walked in, stepped up to the microphone and started screaming his vocals. On another track, 'Rats', Eddie was sitting around watching them play the music, when he started scribbling in his note pad, and then began singing what he had just written.

Gossard was delighted by the extra dynamics that Eddie brought to the band: 'So much of the album arranged itself once he started singing. We'd come down after rehearsing in the studio with some new ideas, and he'd come down later and we'd play him the tape. And he'd say, "Right, let's jam on this riff or that section." Maybe originally we'd played four bars of something, and then with Eddie there we could feel it wanted to go twice as long. You could tell when the music wanted to change just by the way he was singing. It was sort of unspoken.'

Gossard went on to tell *Guitar World* how Eddie further contributed to the new album material: 'If Eddie writes a song, maybe we'll play it exactly like he wrote it – which is essentially what happened with 'Rearviewmirror'. Or if I have a specific song idea, we can do it that way – or we can jam on my idea so there's room for anyone's input. There's an infinite amount of ways we can write songs if we maintain this trust and confidence in each other as a band.' McCready continued, 'People may be surprised to hear that Eddie wrote 'Rearviewmirror' – all the riffs, the whole song. He plays guitar on a couple of tunes, like 'Elderly Woman Behind The Counter In A Small Town', but it sounds like us.' Eddie struggled with 'Rearviewmirror' as he felt it was too 'catchy' for a song about suicide.

This fluidity is what Gossard believes makes Pearl Jam such a potent creative force, and he recognises that Eddie is at this very core: 'It's been a long evolution over a lot of years and bands. First, I had to find my voice as a guitarist, then finally realise that I could write. Eventually you have a different kind of confidence, where you can actually step back from it and say, "Okay, I can do it – and so can everybody else." So, you encourage other people to contribute. And that's what ultimately is going to make this band stand out – if everyone's really comfortable with diving into the creative process . . . in general, I feel the band has opened in a way that allows everybody to continue to explore that creative space.'

• • •

With such a successful debut album, the pressure was really on for Pearl Jam to come up with something special, as Abbruzzese recalled in *Modern Drummer*: 'When we first went into the studio, there wasn't any talk of following up a successful record. We just wanted to make songs that represented us. We didn't want to make Pearl Jam *Eleven*. A lot of the success of the last record did go into the new record, though. I mean, you can't remove yourself from who you are.'

'We're all just souls; everyone wants a chance, and everyone should have one, no matter what colour they are.' *Eddie Vedder*

Eddie most certainly could not remove himself from who he was. The lyrical bent of the new album was similar to that of the first one, but was more intense, more direct, without being bombastic or self-righteous. He talks of the misunderstanding of children with learning difficulties ('Daughter'), which in many ways continued his concern for the rights of youngsters that 'Jeremy' had so startling begun. 'There was a time when they thought that children with learning difficulties were stubborn and selfish,' Eddie told writer Liz Evans. 'It's only recently been recognised for what it is.' He also spits out his venom on the gun culture in America with the angry 'Glorified G', in which he makes crystal clear what he thinks of the stupidity and lame excuses people use for gun possession. He also rants at the white domination of the USA in the real-life inspired 'w.m.a.': 'that stands for white male american. We're all just souls; everyone wants a chance, and everyone should have one, no matter what colour they are.'

Throughout the record Eddie was drawn to voice his concerns about social problems, intertwining his own experience and feelings with events he saw in everyday life. When one writer

*Eddie's recreational drugs are not those necessarily
associated with rock stars.*

put it to him that his words mixed the personal, the political and the spiritual, he replied, 'Well, that's the real things all rolled up. That's just how I am. I've always been that way and I always will be. I just think you have to try and change things – just a bit. I don't really have the power to do much. There's so much more I'd love to do, which has more to do with the real me or whatever. But there's so much you could do, it's insane. I do things, but not publicly – I won't talk about them.'

Musically, the back-drop was far looser than on *Ten.* Strewn with informal count-offs, tangled endings and discordant riffs, the jamming process that underpinned the recording session gave the record a vibrant, organic feel. Less calculated but more rhythmic, less anthemic but perhaps more emotional, the record represented a clear progression. The more economical musical arrangements, and the closer ties between a more dynamic drum and bass, meant that Eddie's vocals, although quite subdued in the mix, took centre stage.

In typical Pearl Jam fashion, and largely because of Eddie, choosing a title for the new album was not an easy matter. Up until about a month before its release, the record was to be called *Five Against One*, as a mark of how the band felt at times about the media frenzy and fan adulation. Then the simpler *Pearl Jam* was mooted, and then finally the even more succinct *Vs.* The confusion and last-minute changes meant that many of the advance copies had no title at all on their sleeves, making them instant collector's items. Full release came in November 1993, by which time *Ten* had sold an incredible five million copies, establishing Pearl Jam as one of the world's leading alternative rock bands. Most people felt it was highly unlikely that they would be able to repeat that level of success. But they didn't just repeat the success, they completely surpassed it.

• • •

In the first week of the new album's release, nearly one million people in America alone went out and bought the record – 950,348 to be more precise. That's over 160,000 every working day – approximately five people every *second*. This smashed the record for the previous fastest-selling album ever, which was Guns N' Roses' *Use Your Illusion II*, coming in with 777,000. To put more perspective on the achievement, Nirvana's highly anticipated third album, *In Utero*, clocked up just over 200,000 in its first week. This achievement was all the more remarkable because of the absence of promotional videos, and the band's apparently minimal collaboration with their marketing department at Epic.

Pearl Jam, once more defying the established norm, had been touring widely before *Vs* was even released, with what the band called 'some fun dates' with Neil Young and U2. Before these they rented out the downtown Moore Theatre in Seattle, for a show that they found so enjoyable they even wrote some new material for the third album immediately afterwards! That was followed by two secret warm-up gigs, in Ament's hometown of Missoula in Montana, and then one in San Francisco. After this, they flew out to Europe to begin the dates supporting the so-called godfather of grunge, Neil Young. He had been impressed by the band when they had played at his annual benefit concert at Bridge Street School the previous year, and backstage at this gig the two camps got on famously. Similarities between the two had frequently been cited, particularly by Pearl Jam's detractors who chided them for being retrogressive, but the band themselves were more than happy to be associated with Young. Right from the opening gig in Norway they found themselves awed by his talent, as McCready told *Guitar Player*: 'Just being able to see Neil Young every night from the front of the stage was amazing, I've never seen better – so tight, but laid-back and groovy too.' Gossard agreed: 'To see some low-key veteran go up there and totally rock and have a good time . . . was a very powerful thing.'

From there, Pearl Jam travelled to Italy to support the ultra-modern U2 in Verona and Rome. For the concert in the capital, Eddie took to the stage with a green T-shirt bearing the gaffer-taped message 'Paul Is Dead' in reference to U2's singer Bono's real name, Paul Hewson (who watched with curiosity from the wings). Eddie also seemed to be trying to stir things up between the two bands when he announced, 'You can't play music in a soccer stadium', and then closed their set by donning a huge fly mask, dancing maniacally as if caught in some monstrous web. Bono, in his own inimitable style, took to the stage and said, 'So you can't play music in a soccer stadium? Well, if you do, it better be good music.' Fortunately, he had clearly not taken Eddie's snipes to heart and by the end of his own set was pronouncing that Pearl Jam were a 'great rock 'n' roll band'. Backstage, any ill feeling was clearly absent as the two bands chatted and mused over the vagaries of fame. Eddie in particular seemed intensely interested in what Bono had to say, taking advice from a man who, after all, had seen everything that the mad world of pop could throw at anyone. Most important of all to Eddie, and the question he kept asking Bono, was how to balance success against integrity. Observers noted how he sounded as if he simply wanted to know how to cope . . .

At the time of Vs*'s release, Pearl Jam collect*
an MTV video award for 'Jeremy'.

Pearl Jam then flew to Ireland for a massive 50,000 seater show at Slane Castle in Dublin, on 10 July, again alongside Neil Young (rumours suggested scalpers were asking $300 a ticket), before launching their official album tour on 28th October at San Francisco's Warfield Theatre. Although hugely successful, this tour was to do much to highlight the difficulties that Pearl Jam were having personally – and, of course, Eddie struggled most of all.

The world's fascination with grunge was reaching rabid proportions. Now hijacked for corporate gain, its original punk ethic and anti-establishment views had been swallowed up by the mass media, by million-dollar marketing and by acceptance into the mainstream of pop. Elevator-music albums included Seattle classics, television chat shows made people over as 'grungers', and, to add insult to injury, fashion designers (mis)appropriated the street style with haute couture copies – Eddie's own corduroy jacket, given to him by Gossard, was the model for one designer's work offered for sale for over $1000. Within eighteen months, grunge would be over and done with, but for now, the world's spotlight seemed to be on its main protagonists, and none more so than Eddie.

The first signs that he was again struggling with his escalating celebrity came in mid-November, when he was arrested on the charge of attacking a waiter in New Orleans. The band were just two weeks into their US tour, and Eddie had been enjoying a quiet drink with support band Urge Overkill and Jack McDowall, pitcher for the Chicago White Sox. They were in a bar in Decataur Street in the city's French quarter, the night after the first of three shows at the Lake Front Arena. At 4am Eddie was arrested on charges of public drunkenness after an alleged brawl with a local, James Gorman. Rumours claimed Eddie spat in the man's face and knocked him unconscious in the street, but the truth was a little less dramatic. The actual details of the scuffle change depending on who you believe, but this is Eddie's version, as he put it angrily to *Melody Maker*: 'What happened was that in New Orleans, somebody did something I didn't like and I spit in their face. And now there's a three million dollar lawsuit. That's fuckin' bullshit. It was like, I was thinking, "Would I take this off this guy if I was just fuckin' anybody?" And I thought, "No, I fuckin' wouldn't." I must have talked to, like, two dozen people that night in that bar and the names of twenty of them ended up on my cocktail napkin plus one for the guest list to our next show. And as far as I remember I talked to this guy for a while . . . and we tried to walk on. But this guy, he wouldn't let it go. He still had to have more. He still had to cover some more points. And Blackie says, 'Look, man, just mellow out, we're going, you know. . .' And this guy's going, "No, no. I got to say one more thing, we gotta talk . . ." and finally I kinda held him against the wall . . . I spit in his face. Big fuckin' deal. Anyway, then all hell broke loose. But I never threw a punch. Thank goodness. Because – who knows? – I could really have hurt him . . . so there's this guy, a talented and well-respected friend of mine who's lying on the ground unconscious because of this little dick who's saying to me, "You're not my Messiah, you're not my Messiah . . ." and I'm going,

"That's what I was trying to tell you, man. That's what I was trying to tell you. I'm not your fuckin' Messiah."' Eddie was bailed for $600 and told to wait to see if he would be fined $500 or face 90 days in jail. Some weeks later, a local judge dropped the charges, much to Eddie's relief.

Within only nine days of this New Orleans fight, Eddie verbally attacked the security at a Colorado gig, whom he thought were being unnecessarily rough with the audience. A summons accusing him of 'obstructing government operations' followed, although nothing came of this matter either. The same could not be said of the next time that Eddie came off the rails, largely because he could not have chosen a more public platform on which to do so. This time he cancelled a scheduled, and much-anticipated, appearance on MTV alongside Nirvana and Soundgarden. The show was due for New Year's Eve at Pier 48 in Seattle, and was to be screened across the entire international MTV network. After the bickering between Pearl Jam and Nirvana, media-fuelled or otherwise, the idea was to reconcile the two bands, who, after all, were fighting on the same side.

Suddenly, the day before the concert, Pearl Jam pulled out. The band's statement said that Eddie's voice was in shreds, and that he was physically exhausted, but the rumour backstage was that he was, in fact, mentally frayed and very ill. Pearl Jam's detractors jumped on this as an example of what they claimed was their lack of substance and queried his health. There was also a host of rumours predicting the impending break-up of the group, citing inter-band tensions and Eddie's increasingly erratic behaviour as the reason. Although tired of such arguments, Eddie was drawn to defend himself in *Melody Maker*. The interview, which is quoted here at length, gives a good insight into the frustrations he was struggling to cope with: 'I was really fuckin' ill, man, and that's the truth. We'd just finished a tour, then we played three more shows in Seattle and I was barely hanging in there. The pressures were intense. They had people lined up in wheelchairs for me to meet and all kinds of shit. And it takes so much out of you, stuff like that, there's nothing left. But I got through that, and then you know what it's like. You get home, and you just totally let your defenses down. It's like letting your guard down in boxing with thirty seconds left in the round and you get fuckin' hit when you least expect it. And I got hit in the face really bad. I was really fucked up. And then they were calling, saying, "Well, can you be

As the 1993 tour progressed it took more and more out of Eddie.

better by Tuesday? Can you do this? Can you do that? Can you play the show?" And I was feeling like shit and I was gonna sound like shit and we knew a lot of people would get to see it if we played and it would sound real shitty. So I just said "no" and it turned out to be a real big fuckin' thing.'

'It bothers you, you try your hardest not to be affected by that stuff, but when people say shit about you without knowing you, it stings.' *Jeff Ament*

On the subject of pulling out for fear of being embarrassed at the hands of Nirvana, Eddie was even more infuriated: 'That was the worst part of it all. Sitting at home fuckin' sick as a dog and sweating and shivering and watching the hours pass before this thing was going to happen and thinking, "I'm fucked, man, I'm totally fucked," and then having it get even worse because there were all these rumours going around about where I was and why I wasn't there. And people were saying we pulled out because we wanted to headline or we wouldn't appear. But fuck it, there was no problem. We would have gone on first, second or fuckin' third, where the fuckever, you know. There was no problem with the order. And I was really happy about playing with them. I even thought about writing to them to say, "Sorry, man, I was sick," but then the rumours got to be fun to listen to. One had me surfing in Hawaii. One had me walking in and seeing all the lights and cameras and going "Whoa, fuck this shit. I'm outta here". . . And that would probably have been the closest to the truth . . .'

These rumours were just a few of the dozens that were swirling around the band at this point, and again Eddie was at their centre. One of the main allegations was that he was an alcoholic – after all, he rarely took to the stage without a bottle of wine, which he invariably swung alongside him throughout the whole set, taking big gulps in between songs. McCready was also rumoured to be drinking heavily, and there was said to be tension between Eddie and the rest of the band, particularly Gossard, who some suggested was on the verge of quitting. Some said Eddie was becoming increasingly reclusive, isolating himself from the band, yet wanting more and more control, the more he retreated. Eddie's increasing withdrawal from media interviews was turned round to make him into an eccentric hermit with ever more anti-social views. Some even believed the tasteless 'Eddie's dead' rumours that cropped up now and then. Ament admitted they were not always able to treat such gossip with the contempt it deserved, as he told *Rolling Stone*: 'It bothers you, you try your hardest not to be affected by that stuff, but when people say shit about you without knowing you, it stings. A lot has changed, and for us to deny that would be ridiculous . . .'

For Pearl Jam, and for Eddie in particular, things would continue to change. Even though the spring tour was more gentle, with dates arranged in short bursts in between informal writing sessions (a horde of new material for the next album was already completed in demo form), he still found it difficult to maintain any perspective. Critics weighed into his on-stage defence of Michael Jackson, who was currently at the centre of allegations of child abuse, as one more example of how the Pearl Jam singer had lost touch.

With his financial security assured for life, and with widespread popular, if not always critical, acclaim, the pressures of fame should have eased on Eddie. However, he recognised himself that he never saw life as that simple. He confided in Gossard during the tour that he related to the late Andrew Wood and his inability to cope, and also described how making his stage performances honest and real was becoming increasingly difficult. For Eddie, with every record they sold, the pressures mounted: 'The whole success thing,' he told *Rolling Stone,* 'I feel like everybody else in the band is a lot happier with it than me. Happy-go-lucky. They kind of roll with it. They enjoy it, even. I can't seem to do that. It's not that I think I'm better than it. I don't know. I'm just not that happy a person. I'm just not. What I enjoy is seeing music, getting to watch. Watching Neil Young. Or I get to watch Sonic Youth from the side of the stage. That's what's been nice for me . . .'

His sentiments were echoed back in Seattle by a single shotgun blast on 8 April 1994, when Nirvana's Kurt Cobain blew his own head off.

CHAPTER EIGHT

'It's just so fuckin' weird. You write about this shit, and you're suddenly the spokesman for a fuckin' generation.'

Eddie

'**T**he shot that was heard around the world' struck at Eddie Vedder's heart like it had been aimed at him. He heard the terrible news with only two weeks of the spring tour to go, while in a hotel room in Washington DC. He sat for a moment in silence then exploded and trashed the room, smashing everything he could lay his hands on, before sitting back on the bed and crying uncontrollably. As he later admitted to the press, his first reaction was, 'I thought I would have gone first.' He said to *Spin,* 'I don't know exactly what was going through his head at that moment or those two weeks or that month or that year. But I definitely have my own set of difficulties, of which I think there are many parallels. And I totally understand. When it happened . . . I just couldn't believe he did it, I couldn't believe he took the step. But I didn't think it was wrong, I just couldn't believe he did it . . . After it happened, I wrote him a letter and asked, "What's on the other side? And is there room for me?"' That night Pearl Jam played a subdued and dour gig in Fairfax, Virginia, and Eddie seemed utterly preoccupied. He rambled in between songs, and said little that was coherent or understandable. The only comment he made clearly about that day's news was to say, 'Sometimes, whether you like it or not, people elevate you . . . it's real easy to fall.'

As the news began to sink in, during the following week Pearl Jam discussed cancelling the remainder of their tour: 'The day that we found out about Kurt, I was just spinning. I was lost and didn't know if we should play, or if we should just go home, or if we should attend the services. I still have some regrets about that, even though in the end it was probably better that we played the last two weeks of the tour. I decided I would play those next two weeks and then I'd never have to play again.' However, by carrying on the band allowed Eddie little time for reflection. Epic were immediately flooded with requests for interviews with Eddie or comments from him, most of which were turned down. However, he did give an interview backstage at the Paramount Theatre in New York, to Allan Jones of *Melody Maker*, in which he exposed the wounds in his psyche that Cobain's suicide had rent open. The harrowing but compelling article, which is possibly the finest piece of writing on Pearl Jam to date, gave an unprecedented insight into Eddie's state of mind: 'I don't know how we've got through this last week. It's been so fuckin' hard, man, so hard . . . I didn't know him on a daily basis – far from it. But, in a way, I don't even feel right being here without him. It's so difficult to really believe he's gone. I still talk about him like he's still here, you know. I can't figure it out. It doesn't make any sense.'

He continued, voice hushed: 'I remember when he got sick in Rome – I didn't realise then that it was actually a suicide attempt – I was in Seattle. I went out to grab something to eat and I saw the headlines. That he was in a coma. I just freaked out, man. I went home and made some phone calls, tried to find out what the fuck was going on. Then I started pacing the house and started to cry. I just kept saying, "Don't go, man, just don't fuckin' go . . . just don't go." I kept thinking, "If he goes, I'm fucked."'

Eddie then attacked the people already circling around Cobain's corpse in judgement: 'Fuck it fuckin' all, you know, all these people man, all lining up to say that his death was so fucking inevitable . . . well, if it was inevitable for him, it's gonna be inevitable for me, too.'

Jones struggled to follow Eddie's erratic train of thought, but still managed to draw some revealing feelings out of him: 'It's just so fuckin' weird. You write about this shit, and you're suddenly the spokesman for a fuckin' generation. Think about it, man, any generation that would pick Kurt or me as its spokesman – that must be a pretty fucked up generation, don't you think? I mean, that generation must be really fucked up, man, really fuckin' fucked up . . .' Eddie slated the press for criticising his 'real' approach and Kurt's honesty, and pleaded to be left alone, saying he had not intended to be seen as a saviour, and doubted whether Kurt did either – he felt they were both 'torn apart' by the public's ludicrous expectations of them. He also said how ridiculous it was to think that pop icons have their lives sorted out when really they are just as 'fucked up' as anyone else. At this stage, he fell silent then smashed a chair against the wall, and started to speculate about the effect the suicide might have on his own band: 'This could be our last show in fuckin' forever as far as I'm concerned. Kurt's death has changed everything. I don't know if I can do it any more.' He went on to talk of not playing music ever again, at least for a long while, and, rather strangely, of living 'in a fuckin' cave with my girlfriend'.

'Think about it, man, any generation that would pick Kurt or me as its spokesman – that must be a pretty fucked up generation, don't you think?' *Eddie Vedder*

At the concert that evening, Eddie remained in a ferociously volatile mood. Coming on after a rendition of Soundgarden's 'Black Hole Sun', he sang like a banshee, losing focus regularly and swearing profusely. He improvised Neil Young's 'Tonight's The Night' at the end of his own track 'Daughter' and then turned to the crowd to say, 'I should just warn you – I'm gonna say "fuck" like about eight times in the next 30 seconds [applause]. Wow it's almost like we didn't even have to play songs – we can just stand up here and say "fuck" . . . lot easier on the throat. This is the last night of the tour – I don't give a fuck about my throat, I don't give a fuck . . . But about that last song, you know . . . If you just feel like saying, "Fuck this, fuck that, fuck everything, fuck you – I'm the fuck outta here . . ." living is the best revenge.'

When one female fan shouted to Eddie that she loved him he snapped nastily back, 'You don't love me, if you really knew me, you wouldn't love me. You love who you *think* I am. And *don't* pretend that you know me. Because I don't even know myself.' The concert had been intended to be a low-key gig for fan club members only – as it turned out it might just have sounded Pearl Jam's death knell.

When asked backstage if he had meant the claim about not

playing again, Eddie did not retract his threat: 'Right now, that's pretty much how I feel, but who knows? Right now, I've just got to get back to Seattle, sort out a lotta shit. I've got to sit down and figure out where to go from here. Everything's just so fuckin' weird, I've got to work it out.'

However, with each day that went by, Eddie seemed to gather increasing perspective on Cobain's death, and it soon emerged that it had, in fact, made him stronger against the evils of the business that only a week before had seemed capable of destroying him. When the band appeared on *Saturday Night Live*, Eddie joined the rest of the cast for the end of the show credits, but instead of shaking hands with the smug Emilio Estevez, he peeled away to the camera and revealed the letter 'K' penned on his T-shirt above his heart, an impromptu memorial to Cobain. Earlier, Eddie had made a similar statement during their performance of 'Daughter', when he had improvised, with two lines from Neil Young's 'Hey Hey, My My (Into The Black)', the song containing the 'it's better to burn out than to fade away' lyric that Cobain had used in his suicide note. Instead of these lines, however, Eddie had sung the equally telling couplet 'Rock 'n' roll will never die, there's more to the picture than meets the eye . . .' Asked why he chose their lines rather than the more famous ones, Eddie said, 'I was just following my emotions at the time. The other lines just meant more to me . . .'

'Right now, I've just got to get back to Seattle, sort out a lotta shit. I've got to sit down and figure out where to go from here.' *Eddie Vedder*

Among his empathies with Cobain on much of what he had found so unbearable, Eddie particularly related to the problem of 'faking it' on stage: 'I had talked to someone at length from two to six in the morning about that same exact dilemma, like two days before Kurt's suicide. When I found out about it, I felt like calling that person and just saying, "Do you see? Do you see what it does?

GERMANY DM 5.30/SPAIN PTS 350/US $3.75

YOUR CULTURE UNDER SIEGE

4-PAGE SPECIAL ON THE
CRIMINAL JUSTICE BILL

M=LODY·MAK=R

E D D I E   O R   N O T

APRIL 30 1994 **75p**

PEARL JAM'S LAST STAND?

'This could be our last show for ever as far as I'm concerned. Kurt's death has changed everything. I don't know if I can do it any more ' — Eddie Vedder

Exclusive report from

New York by Allan Jones

Ride tour dates ● Credit ● Beautiful South ● Wildhearts ● Bark Psychosis ● Lotion

Eddie's despair became headline news in the world's music press.

Do you see?" Because for some reason these complaints from artists are belittled. Somehow they're not taken seriously. Even when you're being honest, they're thinking, "Well, maybe he's tired, or he just wants to go home, or he's calling in sick." I think that's a huge danger. If you go out and play three shows, it's great. If you play 60, somewhere along the line you're going to become an actor, or you're going to have to put yourself on autopilot just to survive it. That pisses me off because it's my fault, because of the songs.' Fortunately, Eddie already seemed able to pull himself out of this circle of self-doubt: 'A lot of times, music is like a wave, so once it starts, you get caught up in it. And if the sound on the stage is good, I can get lost in whatever we're doing, and I'm fine.'

'A lot of times, music is like a wave, so once it starts, you get caught up in it.' *Eddie Vedder*

Once the band were back from the tour, Eddie's reflections were more considered, but no less angry. At first he felt guilty that the two singers had not been closer: 'I wish that Kurt and I had been able to, like, sit in the basement a few nights and just play stupid songs together, and relate to some of this,' he told *Spin*. 'That might've helped us to understand each other, that he wasn't the only one, or that I wasn't the only one . . . we didn't really address that.' Gradually, Eddie gathered resolve – he was no longer a man for whose personal safety you feared, he was stronger than before: 'I think that [healing] process has already begun, seeing what can happen [to Cobain] makes me realise I've got to work on it . . . to avoid getting swallowed up too.' He planned to do this by spending much of the next year ensconced in his basement writing music, and spending time with his girlfriend Beth Liebling. Cameron Crowe, who had cast Eddie in his film *Singles*, was confident he would cope, telling the *Los Angeles Times,* 'I don't think it is going to send him off the deep end. I know he had a lot of those feelings, those impulses himself, and I'm just thinking he was able to almost see what would have happened had he taken that jump . . . and it's not pretty. I think it is going to help strengthen him. I think he'll deal with it properly.' Eddie Vedder had not yet given up the fight even though Pearl Jam withdrew from touring in the wake of the tragedy and would not surface again for over a year.

• • •

As an afternote to the Cobain tragedy, it is worth recalling Courtney Love's reaction to her husband's suicide attempt in Rome, several weeks before he succeeded in taking his own life. Her remark reflects the sometimes unnecessary and vindictive abuse that Pearl Jam, and Eddie in particular, are subjected to. Although the so-called 'feud' between her husband and Eddie had long since subsided, to be replaced by mutual respect, when she heard of her husband's overdose Love is reported to have told the press: 'Why couldn't it have been Eddie Vedder?'

Eddie was known to have been particularly hurt by this, and struggled to understand why someone he had hardly spoken to could bear him such a grudge. In the aftermath of Cobain's suicide, he was still reeling from it: 'That's nice. That's really nice. That makes me feel really good. I wonder why she didn't mention that when I phoned her last night and offered her any help or support I could give her . . . I really don't know any of these people, I don't know Courtney, I'd never talked to her before. But someone said I should call her and I thought maybe I should. I mean, all this shit that comes up and all this bullshit that flies back and forth in the press that gets italicised and trumped up to make it a bigger deal than it really is, when all that's said and done, there's feelings I have for those people. And the ones that are alive, I need to let them know how I feel.'

CHAPTER NINE

FIGHTING THE GOOD FIGHT

'It is a weird position as an artist . . . to blatantly enter the political ring.
We don't come from that space . . . but I know what it is not to be heard.'
Eddie

One way Eddie has always fought the system, the media and just about anyone else he disliked has been through his endorsement of 'good causes'. This has not always been entirely selfless – his desire to challenge himself regularly has helped alleviate the tedium of touring. However, Eddie has been driven by genuine concern on a great spectrum of issues, and has felt deeply engaged with various social problems, many of which he says were first introduced to him through the surfing community. Among the many causes for which Pearl Jam have played benefit gigs, donated royalties, tracks, or been heavily involved in are: People for the Ethical Treatment of Animals, Artists for a Hate Free America, Rock The Vote, Pro Choice, Earth First (a radical environmentalist group, prepared to use illegal means, whose logo of a crossed tomahawk Eddie has tattoed on his calf), anti-pornography campaigns, the Sweet Relief project (to raise funds for country/folk singer, Victoria Williams, who was stricken with multiple sclerosis), Voters For Choice, Move (to educate voters), Surfrider (for the protection of the world's waves and beaches through conservation), the Chicken Soup Brigade (who deliver food and stores for families living with AIDS), JAMPAC (or Joint Artists and Music Promotions Political Action Committee) and even such specific causes as Project, a campaign to raise funds to search for the killer of Mia Zapata, lead singer with the Seattle band the Gits, who was strangled to death in the summer of 1993. Also Jeff Ament and manager Kelly Curtis are directors of AHFA, an organisation designed to raise money to fund groups who fight hate, prejudice and oppression of all kinds.

Two concerts in particular highlight just how involved Eddie allows himself to become in these issues. While observers expected only heavyweight dates to support the *Vs* album, the band chose to play in support of the San Carolos Apache people in their fight to protect their sacred ground, Mount Graham, which also happens to be home to a rich diversity of plant and animal life. In support of the Mount Graham Coalition Group in their opposition to the development of a number of astronomical observatories on the site (funded by the University of Arizona and the Vatican) designed to search for alien life, Pearl Jam played two benefit shows at the start of November 1993, in Mesa, Arizona, and also wrote to President Clinton expressing their anger at the proposal. At the first gig, Eddie walked on stage and said, 'I just spat on a guy's face . . . I just wanted you to know what it felt like . . . you know, the Indians around here have been spat on every day for 400 years.'

Another cause the band, and Eddie in particular, are very vocal in supporting is the fight against the banning of abortion. One of the leading young movements in this fight is Rock For Choice, for whom Pearl Jam have played several benefits, including a notable one in the spring of 1994 in Pensacola, Florida. This part of the Sunshine State is conservatively religious, and popular opinion was strongly against abortion. Eddie had received hundreds of letters from teenagers whose lives had been affected by unwanted pregnancies, and had written back to as many as he could. He felt drawn to take more positive action when he saw the son of the murdered abortion surgeon Dr David Gunn (shot dead by Pro-Lifers on 10 March 1993) on the chat show *Donahue* one evening. Eddie called around various feminist charities, expressing his concern and desire to help, and eventually got hold of Gunn Jr's number. 'Eddie Vedder called me . . . just to say, "Hello and I'm sorry." He genuinely felt bad for me and the situation I was in.'

Eddie offered to organise a benefit tribute in Pensacola in memory of Gunn's father, and at the same time raise awareness of the issues. The actual concert itself fell just four days after the man who shot David Gunn was found guilty of murder, despite leading Pro-Lifers claiming that 'the use of lethal force was justifiable provided it was carried out for the purpose of defending the lives of unborn children'. At the benefit show, Eddie spoke little and carefully, and then introduced David Gunn's son who spoke movingly to the large crowd. Outside a pamphlet, entitled 'Pearl Jam: The Blood', was being distributed which read 'There is only one PEARL worth jammin' out for . . . The "PEARL OF GREAT PEACE" . . . If you continue on the road you are on, rejecting

Jesus Christ . . . you will have a front row seat in the hottest concert in dark, burning, eternal hell. When the doors close you are in forever.'

'If I can raise my hand and speak out for some of these people who don't have a voice at the moment, then I almost feel a responsibility.' *Eddie Vedder*

At a gig in Washington to support the same cause (which Neil Young also played at), Eddie was far more vocal and told a packed press conference: 'It is a weird position as an artist . . . to blatantly enter the political ring. We don't come from that space . . . but I know what it is not to be heard, so if I can raise my hand and speak out for some of these people who don't have a voice at the moment, then I almost feel a responsibility.' He then spoke out against the spate of violence against abortion clinic staff in the US: 'I think it is . . . sickening. There's nothing that distinguishes these people from any other terrorists. I was thinking after David Gunn, which was the first death to come about this way, that everything was going to stop . . . that people were going to realise that Pro-Lifers killing people was going to be the ultimate contradiction and it must stop. As it is, now they're like martyrs.' In another outburst on the subject, Eddie said: 'The thing is, these people don't understand that in these modern times there are too many people here on the boat, and they're trying to tell us to put more people on that boat. The boat is already capsizing, and these people tell me they're concerned with life? Well, so am I! It should be a woman's choice what she does with her body and how she plans her future. If she goes with a guy, why should she be stuck with the problem, and be forced legally to have this baby for the rest of her life, with the responsibility of this child, just because of one fucking dick?!'

Eddie was drawn into writing a piece in *Spin* to explain his intense personal involvement: 'Ten years old. That's the age my child would have been. And I would not be here . . . I wouldn't be in this band or travelling. And I wouldn't have seen the liberal ways in which other countries we have visited deal with this issue.

I wouldn't have been asked to write this piece. Perhaps I'll have a child in the future, when I can provide for properly. Who knows. But as individuals in this "free" country, we must have the right to choose when that time is right . . . This is not a game. This is not a religious pep rally. This is a woman's future.'

Of course, Pearl Jam's detractors loved all this – it smacked of mega-star pomposity, bringing to mind Sting's rainforests and bloated charity concerts. However, Eddie's personal involvement made it clear his concern was genuine. Indeed, he was brave in pursuing these goals when political and social commentary by any band was highly unfashionable. But he saw it as essential to support these many causes, as for him they represented good against evil. He would not let fame or the decision of others make him abandon them.

'The left has a lot to learn from these guys. They need to get organised.' *Eddie Vedder*

In fact, the more money and influence Eddie possessed the more responsible, and even obliged, he felt to back his chosen causes. The 'them and us' mentality was very much evident in this explanation given to *Melody Maker:* 'See, the conservatives are really well-organised, they sit at home watching their church channels, they have letter-writing campaigns and they have a fine network going. The conservatives are using democracy in a supremely active fashion. The left-wing are more passive. They believe no one's gonna take their reproductive rights away, or stop them avoiding pregnancy if they can't afford it. But the left can't afford to think like that any more because these 60-year-old fuckers are organising Pro-Life letter campaigns. Still, they're 60 years old. It's an issue that doesn't concern them anymore. But they're still doing it. The left has a lot to learn from these guys. They need to get organised.' Eddie's commitment and his passion belie the accusations of 'corporate rock' completely.

In an interview with Singapore's *Before I Get Old* magazine, Eddie explained why he was not prepared to stop supporting these issues: 'It's strange because what happens is, I've lived this certain

Eddie's tension contrasts with a laid-back Mike as they prepare for a gig at Red Rock, Denver, Colorado.

life. I've developed certain attitudes towards certain issues. Mostly through education. Other times through personal experience and so I've felt these ways about these issues for years and years and years. Two decades, maybe. And I did things ten years before I've been in this band on much smaller levels. Regarding these same issues, whether it was volunteering or protests and things like that, my girlfriend, my wife now, we would go to these things. We would be in the front line of these issues. It's still the same. We're still the same people with the same ideals. But now a whole lot of people are paying attention. So what am I gonna do? Pretend that I don't have those ideals? I mean, the Beatles were told not to mention the Vietnam War the first two times they came to America. They had to kind of joke their way around the issues. I'm sure that made them pretty sick and in the end they decided they had to make their honest statement. So you find yourselves in some very strange positions where your life is in jeopardy.'

'. . . if you get lost in these individual situations and circumstances, if you get too drawn in, you can lose control of your own life and where you're going'.

Eddie Vedder

While Eddie was throwing himself into his causes whole-heartedly, people around him worried about the toll they were exacting on him. He always seemed to take things more to heart than his bandmates, and his manager had long since decided to vet the letters that fans sent to Eddie. Many times he had found Eddie late at night in his office poring over desperately sad letters, trying to think of ways to help. Occasionally, people even came to his house, desperate for advice. Sometimes he took action, such as when he received a letter from a thirteen-year-old boy whose father had left him and his mother. She had to bring up three children on her own, working by cleaning toilets and delivering post to bring in barely enough money. She also saved what spare cash she had to enroll in a community college, where she eventually gained a degree. Then as the world of opportunities and higher paid jobs opened up before her, she had an accident and her hip was smashed so badly she could no longer walk or work. On Valentine's Day of the year the boy wrote to Eddie, she had tried to kill herself. Eddie would not reveal the help he provided but he was deeply affected by this dreadful situation.

However, Eddie knew he was wearing himself down, and came to recognise the dangers if he couldn't pull himself away: 'We're constantly getting letters asking us to do this or do that. And they're good causes. But they can't even show them to me any more, because they know I'll let my innards be scooped out. I'll have nothing left. And people have advised me on this. They've said, "What you're doing musically, don't jeopardise that. The music is something everyone can get something out of, and you shouldn't be required to do anything more. And if you put everything into that, then that's helping more people than you could ever imagine."' He continued in this interview in *Melody Maker*: 'And I've come to realise that these people are probably right. Because if you get lost in these individual situations and circumstances, if you get too drawn in, you can lose control of your own life and where you're going. And then you really would be worthless as far as making music and in the end you need to protect that. So as far as all these cries for help go, it's easy to hear and easy to take in. But it's almost impossible to do anything. And that may be really fuckin' hard to accept, but it's the sad fuckin' truth.' He also said, ominously, 'What they don't understand is that you can't save somebody from drowning if you're treading water yourself . . .'

CHAPTER TEN

LOSING BATTLES

'If it all ends tomorrow, I will be the happiest fucking gas-station attendant you ever saw.'

Eddie

Despite the record-breaking success of *Vs*, much of the period after its release would be remembered for yet another side-issue that Eddie became embroiled in, this time with the full co-operation of his band mates. Pearl Jam's lengthy and at times vicious battle with the industry's largest ticket agency, Ticketmaster, would alter their lives and fortunes indelibly and forever.

The essence of the dispute with Ticketmaster was actually very simple, although the details and the ramifications for both Pearl Jam and the music industry were complex. Firstly, Pearl Jam objected to the vastly inflated prices being asked for concert tickets. Some prices for mainstream acts like the Eagles, Elton John and Rod Stewart had topped $100, and even for the more alternative bands, prices were sometimes as high as $50. Secondly, they resented the so-called 'service charge', which the agency added to the cost of the ticket for administration. In some instances this had been as high as $15 but there appeared to be no consistency to the way it was calculated. Thirdly, they claimed the agency should print how much of the face value of the ticket was a service charge, which was not then the case. Fourthly, Pearl Jam objected to the advertising on some tickets. Fifthly, they claimed that since their 1991 buy-out of nearest rival Ticketron, Ticketmaster had effectively held an unhealthy and potentially illegal monopoly on the industry (with approximately 80 percent of US venues), which in turn effected a restraint of trade on both bands and promoters. A final allegation was that Ticketmaster had instigated an underhand boycott of the band when Pearl Jam had tried to lay on a cheaply-priced tour in the summer. One memorandum that was circulated allegedly to prevent this called the agencies, with masonic-style clubiness, "brother raccoons". Ticketmaster denied all the allegations completely.

Eddie had this to say of the controversy in *Spin*: 'We don't want to exclude anybody from the experience. The experience of a father taking his son to the concert even though he works at a gas station . . . or even being able to afford a T-shirt. What music can do to your life, what one night of live music, if all the elements are in place, how it can affect your life. It might make this kid pick up a guitar. Who knows what it will do.'

'The high price of concert tickets – especially the imposition of excessive service charges – is a significant issue to us and we believe to the public generally.' *Stone Gossard and Jeff Ament*

Confrontations between the two parties led inextricably towards a shoot-out. The first difficulties were at the 'Drop In The Park' show in 1992, which was intended to be a free show to replace the cancelled Gasworks concert. Pearl Jam were to pay the $100,000 costs of staging the show, but were angered when Ticketmaster refused to distribute tickets for less than $1.50 each. Pearl Jam rejected these terms and used other arrangements.

Next up was a disagreement in December 1993 at a Seattle Center Arena charity show. Pearl Jam claimed Ticketmaster had agreed to donate $1 per ticket to charity, only to then raise the service charge by the same amount. They also claimed the agency later reneged on an agreed lump sum donation.

By now the atmosphere was openly hostile, and in Chicago and Detroit in 1994, confrontations occurred over declaring the service charge – in Detroit ticket-printing machines were deliberately disabled by Ticketmaster as Pearl Jam were planning to use them to sell non-Ticketmaster tickets. This was against a backdrop of what Pearl Jam claimed was intimidation by Ticketmaster, both legal and otherwise, against promoters and industry people who backed or dealt with Pearl Jam. In some cases, promoters were warned they would face hefty law suits if they reneged on their exclusive contracts. In one instance, a promoter was allegedly told to watch his back. In such an aggressive and unworkable atmosphere, the remainder of the *Vs* tour had to be cancelled, at a cost to the band of around $3 million.

The heavyweight United States Department of Justice heard about Pearl Jam's problems and in May 1994 contacted the band (not, as common myth has it, the other way around). After lengthy conversations they decided to launch an enquiry into the agency's affairs with regard to possible anti-trust charges. So, on 30 June 1994, Stone Gossard and Jeff Ament found themselves in the rather musty environment of a Congressional Subcommittee on Information, Justice, Transportation, and Agriculture, testifying for three hours against Ticketmaster.

During their lengthy statement, Gossard and Ament stated that Ticketmaster were 'unlawfully interfering with our freedom to determine the price and other terms on which tickets to our concerts will be sold. The high price of concert tickets – especially the imposition of excessive service charges – is a significant issue to us and we believe to the public generally.' They also said, 'We believe Ticketmaster's business practices violate the anti-trust laws and the consequences those business practices have on us, on our fans, and on others who purchase tickets to concerts,' and that they 'do not want to be responsible for teenagers, who may be influenced by peer pressure to feel that they must see Pearl Jam perform'. They summed up by saying Ticketmaster has effectively thwarted competition and left most bands without any meaningful alternative for distributing tickets. This absence of any alternative, in turn, gave Ticketmaster the power to exercise 'virtual control'.

Ticketmaster denied everything. Their notoriously hard-nosed Chief Executive Officer, Fred Rosen, vehemently reiterated that he believed it was his right to compete aggressively, and they forwarded two sharp-shooting lawyers to represent their case at the Congressional Subcommittee. They claimed the quality of service had improved enormously since they had become the leading agency, and they dismissed Pearl Jam's accusations as unrealistic and equally restrictive. Actions such as threatening law suits and closing down box offices and ticket machines were simply in order to protect their hard-earned, contractually-bound, market share. As for the exclusive contracts, they claimed that no-one was forced to sign anything. Ticketmaster said they had openly stated their intentions to Pearl Jam. The band recounted that they had been informed Ticketmaster would 'aggressively enforce their contracts with promoters and facilities. Ticketmaster's stance is that they have been loyal to their partners in this business and they hope and expect their partners will reciprocate' and that the agency 'will use all available remedies to protect itself'.

During the heat of battle, several key players joined forces with Pearl Jam. REM were the first big-name ally, and they were swiftly followed by Neil Young, the Grateful Dead, and the mega-selling country artist Garth Brooks. Aerosmith also joined up, and their participation led to the most incisive comment on Ticketmaster's attitude, when lead singer Steve Tyler said, 'Mussolini may have made trains run on time but not everyone could get a seat on those trains.' Pearl Jam's cause was not helped, however, by the media, especially the tabloids, who treated their appearance on Capitol Hill as a novelty – scruffy grunge-rockers holding court with the government – and in many publications the real issue was completely lost.

Eventually signs that the fight was going against Pearl Jam started to appear. REM signed up with Ticketmaster for the massive world tour to promote their huge *Monster* album. 'I don't like Ticketmaster,' guitarist Peter Buck told the *Chicago Tribune*, 'but I am not going to not tour. I'm not going to cripple my band because society is not run the way I like it.' Aerosmith also signed on the dotted line with the enemy. With admirable honesty, their manager Tim Collins told *Billboard* that he could not take on the agency like Pearl Jam had and that 'we weren't in a position of not touring, I mean, how many years does Aerosmith have left?'

For over a year, the Subcommittee interviewed tour staff, artists, managers, other agency workers and promoters. Then on 5 July 1995 with much of the capital quiet in the aftermath of Independence Day, the Subcommittee destroyed Pearl Jam's hopes with a simple two-sentence statement that stated they had found no reason to continue their enquiries. Put simply, Ticketmaster had won. The agency smugly issued a statement which said, 'Getting attacked by a superstar rock band is a lot like being accused of kicking your dog: There's a general presumption of guilt until proven innocent. Luckily the facts were on our side, and we prevailed.'

However, there were some repercussions for the giant agency. The bad press had raised public awareness of their

Mike McCready observes the dwindling queues for tickets . . .

back-door dealings, and the emergence of a handful of lower-priced tickets and cheaper deals with some alternative bands heralded a victory of sorts for Pearl Jam. 'I'm not sure it helped Pearl Jam,' David Sestak, co-manager of Live told *Rolling Stone*, 'but it definitely helped the consumers.' Also, a number of small law suits were filed by customers of Ticketmaster along the same lines as Pearl Jam's complaints. However, the war had been won by the agency. Worse still, there were signs that Pearl Jam might never recover from the wounds inflicted during the battle.

• • •

'It was the final insult as to how blown out of proportion that thing got,' Pearl Jam's manager Kelly Curtis told the *San Jose Mercury News,* 'because we were just talking about a few dollars per ticket, and it was just one more very, very, very small detail of how we handle our shows. Maybe we shouldn't have worried about it, but at least we were consistent.' Although the band's daring stance would result in lower ticket sales, Harvey Leeds, Vice President of promotion at Epic, backed them up despite the defeat: 'I've never in my twenty years seen an act this sensitive to their fan base.' Other observers disagreed, saying that Eddie's obsession with Ticketmaster had caused him to lose focus. *Rolling Stone* quoted 'the manager of a multi-platinum rock act' as saying, 'Obviously, Eddie is attuned to the evils of the business, but how many of your fans really give a fuck? The majority of them don't. They don't care if it's in venue X, Y or Z, or what the ticket

'I've never in my twenty years seen an act this sensitive to their fan base.' *Harvey Leeds*

company is. They want to hear you play good music.'

Eddie Vedder's only real public comment on the entire affair was to compare the Justice Department's decision to the shoddy process of law the US had recently seen during the Rodney King trial that had led to the LA riots: '. . . the justice we saw in the trial in LA. You can hire people and make it work. That's what they did. They had the dream team.'

The first the public heard of Pearl Jam after their June 1994 visit to Congress was when it was announced that drummer Dave Abbruzzese had left the group. Manager Kelly Curtis said in a brief statement that it was because Abbruzzese wished to 'study music formally'. However, a few days later, the drummer denied this and claimed to have no clue to the reasons for his dismissal.

Insiders said Abbruzzese had never fully fitted in, that he was always too comfortable with the benefits of fame and fortune, and

'There's a lot of intensity over decisions, and I think it's great. But every once in a while, I wish everyone would just let it go.' *Dave Abbruzzese*

that he often riled the rest of the band, particularly Eddie. In band meetings Abbruzzese would ask, 'What's the next single then?', a harmless enough question in most groups, but one which drew scowls of derision from his colleagues. The degree to which he was at odds with his bandmates had been there to see in interviews: 'To me, when I was younger,' he once told *Rolling Stone,* 'and I heard about a band selling a million records, I thought the band would get together and jump up and down for at least a minute and just go, "Wow, I can't believe it." But it doesn't happen that way [in this band]. Me, I flip out. I jump up and down by myself.' He also said, 'There's a lot of intensity over decisions, and I think it's great. But every once in a while, I wish everyone would just let it go. Make a bad decision!' Eddie struggled with this more relaxed outlook; when they recorded *Vs* at the Site, while he was trekking over the hills around San Francisco desperate to get away from the plush surroundings, Abbruzzese loved them, calling the studio 'paradise'. One insider said Abbruzzese's eagerness to talk to the media was also a major stumbling block: 'Dave was too much of a rock star. He was giving cover-story interviews to drumming magazines. He was happy, he was achieving his dream. That bugged the fuck out of Eddie. I witnessed Eddie drawing mustaches on Dave's face on the cover of *Modern Drummer.*'

Sources close to the band claimed that Eddie was the main

instigator of the sacking, and such was his authority in Pearl Jam by now that no-one dared argue. But he was not the only one who felt that Abbruzzese's time in the band had to come to an end: 'It's a very complex scenario,' said Gossard in *Musician* magazine 'and certainly Dave was, and is, not the only person in Pearl Jam with personality flaws. Everybody in this band exhibits some form of neurotic behaviour. And we couldn't find a balance, a mutual respect for each other. Because of that, nobody was really playing with their hearts as open as they could be . . . I think your artistic style and your personality are very interrelated. Dave played an important part in our growing, but change occurs.'

After Gossard told him the news of his dismissal in August 1994, Abbruzzese joined a band called Green Romance Orchestra.

• • •

While all eyes had been on Eddie Vedder, Mike McCready had been plummeting into alcoholism and drug abuse. After the tour for *Vs* finished, he admitted his problem, went into rehab and emerged clean and sober. With admirable openness he told *Guitar World* how these problems had affected both his private and professional life: 'We had a lot of meetings where they would say, "Hey Mike, you're getting way too fucked up." But we're all really good friends and we love each other and I think they actually thought I was going to die, but they never took steps to kick me out of the band, which I can't believe because I fucked up so many times. I'd clean up for a little while then I'd fall off the wagon, like addicts do. They called me all the time, and it was cool because I really needed their support. They're my greatest friends. Eddie and I have been kind of distanced from each other over the past couple of years because of my condition. I didn't have a lot of confidence; I was literally afraid of everybody. I didn't know how to relate to Eddie, and after the band really took off, I went off in my own world. When I started getting clean I told Eddie, "Listen, man, I know I've been fucked up for a long time, but I want to re-establish the relationship that we had in the beginning."' McCready was also realistic about the second chance he had been given: 'It's just one day at a time. I want it to be over. I don't want to go back to feeling like shit every single day of my life and blacking out. If I go back, I'm gonna die.'

The tensions that McCready felt were echoed by similar

difficulties within the rest of the band, not least Eddie. Although McCready felt under pressure, he had feared for Eddie: 'People don't know Eddie. He's one of the most caring individuals I've ever met in my life, if not *the* most caring. He's very intelligent. I think he gets freaked out about people following him around.

Dave Abbruzzese was happy with the glamour of rock star success.

Honestly, I don't know what he has to go through. The level that I'm on is very strange to me, and he's got the same thing . . . only twenty times more so. He can't really go out in public, which has to fuck with your head. He's not bitching for the sake of bitching; he just needs his peace.' So when McCready got out of rehab, the band sat down and discussed where they were going, if Pearl Jam was still worth keeping alive, and how or if they could still get on. They decided they could, and they decided they still wanted to perform and record.

CHAPTER ELEVEN

VITALOGY

'There's no doubt about where it's coming from. It's straight from inside you, and that's fulfilling, because it's therapeutic.'

Eddie

Among all the distractions, it was easy to forget that Pearl Jam were actually a band. They appeared so preoccupied at times with other issues that the music seemed to take a back-seat, in a direct contradiction to what Eddie had always wanted. So it was with much relief in some quarters when it became apparent that the band had knuckled down to recording their third album, entitled *Vitalogy*. Slated for release in late December 1994, it was made before Abbruzzese's dismissal. Despite everything that had happened, the new record was comfortably their best yet.

Unlike its two predecessors, this album was recorded in a variety of places, spread over a period of time. Much of the work was done while the band were on the road, and that alone gave the record a very different feel to the first two albums. They recorded some material at Bad Animals Studios in Seattle, at the very end of the *Vs* tour, then they later spent time working in New Orleans and Atlanta. Much of the material was written at soundchecks, which were unusually intense. To complement the new tunes, Eddie brought out some old songs from his pre-Pearl Jam days. The actual writing process was the most democratic Pearl Jam had produced, with Gossard stepping back and letting the others contribute much more heavily. Also, the record was completed in the immediate aftermath of Kurt Cobain's suicide, and that was to impose a great weight on the project.

Initially, McCready worried that such a disparate evolution, in these circumstances, would make the record an incoherent, listless affair. Part of this reservation was the band's current inability to communicate with each other, as Gossard later explained to *Musician* magazine: 'It really is more of an Eddie record in terms of his influence playing guitar, for instance. The record was symptomatic of the band's state. In fact, it was probably the only record we could have made due to the problems we were going through in relating. We really weren't collaborating with each other at the time very much. So the only way we could make something happen was by going into the studio and deciding on it then and there, in the moment. Eighty percent of the songs were written twenty minutes before they were recorded . . . most of the songs were a result of jamming in the studio and coming up with a quick arrangement. It felt like what we needed to do to really break the band open.'

'We really weren't collaborating with each other at the time . . . So the only way we could make something happen was by going into the studio and deciding on it then and there.' *Stone Gossard*

McCready remained unconvinced, even after the album had been mastered, but he needn't have worried. *Vitalogy* was far from incoherent. It was complex, yes, and hard listening too. There were also tracks which were decidedly inferior. However, when the album made sense, it was a deep, emotional, musically rich tapestry, despite its occasional abstruse flavour. Thematically the album touched on the media, the family, betrayal, responsibility, and emotional anger. Nothing new for the band perhaps, but the way Eddie dealt with these songs was far superior to what they had done before.

In order to get inside Eddie's mind at work, it is interesting to look at this album in depth, to see how much thought goes into his work, where he gets his inspiration, how much he changes things, and what he feels during that process. The opening 'Last Exit' touches on the subject of death, the first word on the lyric sheet being 'die'. Elsewhere, in 'Immortality', the spectre of Kurt's death seems to loom large, although Eddie was not about to play on this: 'No, that was written when we were on tour in Atlanta,' he told the *Los Angeles Times.* 'It's not about Kurt. Nothing on the album was written directly about Kurt, and I don't feel like talking about him, because it might be seen as exploitation. But I think there might be some things in the lyrics that you could read into and maybe will answer some questions or help you understand the pressures on someone who is on a parallel train.' Even the reference in the song to a cigar box, like the one which was found next to Cobain's corpse, was passed off as being to one where Eddie often kept his tapes. All the same, Eddie must have known people would assume this track referred to Kurt.

The new, harder Pearl Jam were again present on the next track, the punk-like 'Spin The Black Circle', which is almost thrash, a twisted love song about Eddie's love for vinyl records. However, Eddie seemed to be veering off to the bizarre, with the liner notes talking of CDs as bad acid. The following song, 'Not For You', was more obvious – a clear-cut attack on the media and executives in it. Eddie said in the *Los Angeles Times:* 'There is something sacred about youth, and the song is about how youth is being sold and exploited. I think I felt like I had become part of that too. Maybe that's why sometimes I have a hard time with the TV end of music and much of the media and the magazines. When I pick up a magazine, I just count how many pages of ads before the first article starts. You go one, two . . . up to fifteen to twenty or more. And then in the back you have phone sex ads. So I've pretty much had it. I don't want to be the travelling medicine show where we go out and do the song and dance and someone else drops the back of the wagon and starts selling crap. I don't want our music to sell anything – or anyone else use it.' At the same time, he enjoyed the evolution of this track, saying, 'there's no doubt about where it's coming from. It's straight from inside you, and that's fulfilling, because it's therapeutic.'

'Tremor Christ' was another song from within: 'We recorded [that] in a very short period, one night in New Orleans, and I remember what that night was like. I can see how the lights were turned down low. I can see the room. And so I like listening to that.' Next up was the album's stand-out track, 'Nothingman', which was written even more quickly, in just over an hour. Eddie had recently married his long-term partner, Beth Liebling. Held during a break from touring, their very private ceremony was conducted in the Prazza del Campidoglia in Rome, in the last week of July 1994. Eddie wrote 'Nothingman' just before the wedding, and it was perhaps Pearl Jam's most obvious ballad yet, but it worked beautifully: 'I might bring something I know from the relationship to 'Nothingman', but I'm thinking about someone else going through it, someone who fucked up. I didn't fuck up. The idea is about if you love someone and they love you, don't fuck up . . . 'cause you are left with less than nothing. Relationships can be tough. There are times – I end up putting a lot of time into this music thing. I don't sleep at night. I think I'm probably a very difficult person to deal with. Things never seem to settle down and be normal, and I think that Beth has to deal with a lot. I don't want to get into our personal relations. But at times there is a tension. We are all selfish at heart, I guess. But I just know that without her, I'd be a kite without a string, a nothing man.' He also said in *Spin*, 'It just happened and somehow captured a mood there, at least for me in the vocal. Any time I can nail down a song, a thought, in a half hour, that feels really good.'

Another song about relationships was 'Corduroy', which Eddie was keen to point out was not about him and Beth either: 'It is about a relationship but not between two people. It's more one person's relationship with a million people. In fact, that song's almost a little too obvious for me. That's why instead of a lyric sheet we put in an X-ray of my teeth from last January and they are all in very bad shape, which was analogous to my head at the time.' Eddie's humour, which is something that is generally missed, was also allowed an outlet on the record, in 'Bugs'. This bizarre, heavy-going track was slated by many critics, but it was merely a tongue-in-cheek bit of fun. Eddie told the story of the song's creation to *Spin*: 'Before I went in the studio, I was walking around some little thrift shop, I found an accordion. And I went in with the accordion and played something, and then spoke some gibberish over the top. I remember laughing and saying, "That's the first single." I think that it's almost confidence that enables us to record 'Bugs', or confidence in our listeners that they can open up to something like that. Back then [with *Ten*] I had my mind on the business at hand, and I probably wouldn't have felt so free to take up two hours of studio time working on Eddie's wank-off accordion piece. For a long time after recording it, I was playing it for friends saying it was the best thing we'd ever done. We just decided to do something that was fun to listen to and wasn't bombastic and wasn't everything that the band had become.'

Unfortunately, things didn't come off with 'Pry, To', where Eddie spelt out the word 'privacy' over and over. Despite being only a minute long it was tedious. Not that this could be said about 'Better Man', another stand-out track about failed love. This was a song Eddie had written ten years before, sitting on his bed with a cheap four-pack (he was not even old enough to drink at the time). Despite his lack of fame back then, he felt it said a lot about people's overblown expectations of rock stars: 'You know the truth. You know that you're just a normal guy. You know you're not even that good. You know that anybody could do what you're doing. The kind of writing I do now is like what I've always done. I really feel that way. I didn't have lessons. I just do something I like to do.'

This track utilised a different narrative approach from songs like 'Nothingman': 'There are times like "Better Man" where you are creating a fictional character – the way James Taylor does in,

After a relationship of several years, Eddie and Beth Liebling
get married quietly in Rome.

say, "Mill Worker" – and working within the framework of someone else's head. That's really fulfilling because you feel like you are writing a story.' In this case, it was the tale of a woman in yet another bad relationship, almost akin to 'Elderly Woman Behind The Counter In A Small Town' on *Vs*. 'Better Man' was the album's simplest, most haunting song in many ways.

Another experiment was 'Aye Davanita', this time into the realms of tribal dance, with native drumming, bulbous bass lines and surreal guitar sweeps complimenting the peculiar chanting which underpins the song. Also known as 'Song Without Words' this three-minute instrumental really was Pearl Jam throwing off all their retro accusations

On the last track of the album, the bizarre 'Stupidmop', Eddie exposed the darkest corners of his mind in a deeply unsettling seven-minute closure. Made from taped loops of strained voices and wailing guitars, the track opens with a young girl talking of spanking being better than hugs, of closeness, and of suicide. The track closes with the girl being asked a question that no-one dared ask in the wake of Cobain's suicide – 'Do you ever think that you might kill yourself?' to which she replies, 'Well, if I thought about it real deep, I believe I would.' The track smacks of experimentalist Beatles and weird sixties studio trickery, and was completely outside anything Pearl Jam had done before. Alongside the confusion of 'Aye Davanita', 'Pry, To' and 'Bugs', it at least showed that the band were not prepared just to produce formulaic rock.

After Cobain's suicide, making the album could easily have been traumatic for Eddie, but it appeared he had put this to one side and dealt with the issues from his own point of view. He clearly had been dwelling on what his songs brought to people: 'I thought about this last night,' he told *Spin*. 'I saw this soul singer who told me how people come up to him and say how they have fallen in love to his music, and that they romanced to his music. It was a very nice thing. I thought, what a huge relief to have someone tell you that rather than "I was going to commit suicide until I heard your song," or "We played your music at my friend's funeral." Fame is so different for different people.'

Eddie's intense involvement in every aspect of *Vitalogy* extended to producing the concept for the artwork. Containing no plastic, the packaging was a beautifully printed booklet with gold lettering, inspired by a book that Ament had discovered in an old junk store. It was this book that also accounted for the odd title. Ament's find was a home health encyclopedia called *Vitalogy* which was first published in 1899, and which by 1930 had sold over a million copies. It contained chapters on anatomy, diseases, cures, and sexuality, all of which Eddie loved browsing through, looking at the odd remedies and out-of-date explanations. He combined a selection of lyrics from the album and musings (such as a petition protesting against the Pro-Life murder of Dr Gunn) with artwork from the original *Vitalogy*, making a unique package. Of course, the extra costs were enormous, reportedly over $2,000,000, but the band readily agreed to chip in for their expensive designs.

Considering the diverse and difficult nature of the new album, it could have been expected to struggle to compete with the phenomenal success of its predecessors. Remarkably, though, in its first week of release, the CD of *Vitalogy* sold a massive 877,000 copies, a figure which would have been even higher but for Pearl Jam's having released the vinyl version two weeks previously (in the process making it the first vinyl album to chart in the *Billboard* Top 100, at Number 55, since the widespread acceptance of CD). It seemed that the Ticketmaster troubles, the lack of videos, and the myriad distractions the band had undergone since the release of *Vs* only thirteen months before, had had no impact whatsoever on the band's huge popularity. Even more notably, the sales of *Vitalogy* remained high for many months, despite the band's usual refusal to record promotional videos. The only concession to Epic was the release of their first ever US single, the far-from-radio-friendly 'Spin The Black Circle'. Even this was done with their fans in mind, with the band citing the high prices they were being asked to pay for European singles made available on import. This was, however, the only chink in Pearl Jam's increasingly anti-commercial armour.

The success of *Vitalogy* was in the teeth of another obstacle placed in its way by the band – a decision not to give press interviews to support it. This decision to spurn the entire music press came out of years of exasperation at the way the band had been treated, and from Eddie's increasing wariness of the media's motives. While the multitude of attacks by the press on himself and his band were the main reason for the decision there were others – when Eddie appeared on 99.9FM KISW Radio in Seattle and was asked about the press, his rambling reply dwelt on the feeling that they were being exploited by the media and that the attendant celebrity misrepresented them: 'Isn't it strange the way that everybody picks up on something and squeezes the juice out of it until there's nothing left. There, I have to say, that it is a little bit of exploitation going on and I mean if bands like us are music, and young kids, and drops outs, etc., are being put on the cover of *Time* magazine, I mean, you just might look at that and go, "Wow, *Time* magazine." But did you ever think that all they're really trying to do is sell magazines by putting the newest rage on the cover?' Eddie continued his rant, barely stopping for breath: 'Believe me, we never thought we'd be in this position. It would have just been a joke had someone told me this before. Do people who listen to music, do you not catch on to that? That the bands really have nothing to do with that and the bands don't have anything to do with the exposure and that? We need your trust on that. I mean, this is nothing that we actually set out to do. We set out to make music and you know, it's nice to be heard, umm, but we don't want people to stop listening to us 'cause we're the latest big thing or we're part of the establishment, etc., which we won't be. You know, we may have money now, we don't act like rich men . . . [The music is] art. That's what I'm married to. I'm not married to the thought of any kind of stardom or mass popularity . . . that is something that makes me uneasy.'

There was also an element of Eddie's feeling unworthy of the attention that was being showered on him. He knew, of course, that he would never be able to pursue the utterly anti-mainstream line that Ian MacKaye of Fugazi or, to a lesser extent, Henry Rollins did, much to their credit, and this drew pangs of guilt. 'I can be around somebody from a band like Mudhoney, or I think about a band like Gas Huffer or a band like the Fastbacks, and I feel like, why aren't they reaping the benefits of success? That's just one facet, one cut on the diamond of which there's a myriad of negative emotions that I seem to be dealing with. I'm really having a difficult time sifting out any positives.'

The drummer chosen to replace Dave Abbruzzese brought Pearl Jam back full circle: Jack Irons, the man who had recommended Eddie Vedder to Stone Gossard way back when the band first started. Irons had already left the Chili Peppers before he made his first fully-visible public appearance with Pearl Jam at a Voters For Choice Benefit gig in Washington DC on 14 January 1995. This was the band's first show for nearly a year, as well as their first public concert since starting their campaign against Ticketmaster. Tickets were sold through an elaborate mail lottery, which received an incredible 167,000 requests for seats. Abbruzzese had been very popular with dedicated fans, partly because many saw him as far more accessible than the sometimes aloof Eddie. So when new boy Jack Irons took to the stage, a loud chorus of boos whistled around the arena. Eddie was quick to pounce on this, saying, 'I heard a few boos out there . . . and I know you were thinking of Dave and that's cool, [but] believe it or not, Jack Irons saved the life of this band . . . so thank him.' Ament told the press now they felt at ease with the new drummer: 'Whether we're together for two more months or ten more years or twenty more years – it feels like the definitive right version of this band because Jack had a lot to do with us finding Eddie. I'm ready to be in a band again. Hopefully, we can work out our ticketing thing. We'll figure it all out, and then we can play.'

Irons had made his debut some days earlier on what Pearl Jam dubbed Self-Pollution Radio. Once again, this was a brainwave of Eddie's, the idea being to broadcast leading alternative bands on their own pirate radio, from Eddie's rather dilapidated house. In a somewhat bizarre setting, the four and a half hour show started with Eddie tapping the microphone and saying, 'Hey . . . am I on?' Thereafter, a whole host of top names called round to join in – it was like a Seattle reunion party. Live sets from Pearl Jam, Soundgarden, Mudhoney, the Fastbacks and Mad Season (a side project for Pearl Jam's Mike McCready and Alice In Chains' Layne Staley) complemented a spoken word set from former Nirvana bassist Krist Novoselic and preview tracks from former Nirvana drummer Dave Grohl's new Foo Fighter's album. Bands played the live sets in the bedroom, and the DJ gear was stored in a separate trailer outside. Occasionally Eddie found himself caught out and had to run through his bedroom out to the DJ desk outside. The band had bought the satellite time (at $350 an hour), and the equipment they needed, and made the show available on a non-exclusive basis to any radio station that wanted to carry it – over 60 did. Krist Novoselic told *Rolling Stone* how much he enjoyed himself: 'Everybody looks happy and healthy tonight. It's like a community thing. It's fantastic!' Soundgarden's Matt Cameron was even keener, saying, 'I think this should happen every week!' Indeed, other broadcasts by Self-Pollution Radio followed, supported by Epic both financially and in principle, who figured if Pearl Jam wouldn't release videos then any promotion was welcome.

CHAPTER TWELVE

SPONSORED BY NO ONE

'I needed a sick day, and you can't necessarily do that in this job. There are 50,000 people, and they've all come to this place, and – oh, it was just brutal.'

Eddie

The start of the *Vitalogy* tour was a sporadic affair, with the band mixing occasional live dates with other related events. To kick it off, they played a secret show under the pseudonym Piss Bottle Men at the Moore Theatre in Seattle. The gig was designed as a rehearsal-cum-free-show for the band's fan club members. Although it was clear that the new record was far more proto-punk than anything the band had previously done, the live renditions proved much harder, with songs like 'Spin The Black Circle' verging on thrash.

Next they were involved in the induction of their now-close friend Neil Young into the Rock And Roll Hall Of Fame at New York's Waldorf Astoria Hotel in January 1995. Having been around for nearly three decades, Young had come to be seen by the new generation as 'the Godfather of grunge' and it was with this in mind that Pearl Jam were asked to present him with his accolade. At the same award ceremony, Led Zeppelin, Frank Zappa, Janis Joplin, Al Green and the Allman Brothers were also inducted. Young performed a one-off collaboration with Robert Plant and Jimmy Page while Eddie stood backstage spitting grape pips at photographers.

The world tour proper kicked off abroad at the end of February 1995, when the band flew to the Far East to play shows in the Philippines, before going on to Australasia. At one of the gigs in Manila, the crowds of fans without tickets outside the venue became so irate that riot police had to be called and tear gas fired off. Unfortunately, crowds were no less turbulent in Australia and New Zealand, where fanaticism for the band continued unabated. A crowd crush in Sydney's Myers Music

Bowl led to over 50 people being hurt, and police were forced to let in thousands of ticketless fans to avoid further injury. Away from the gigs, Eddie himself had a close shave when he was swimming off the coast of New Zealand's Karekare Beach and got into trouble when the tide swept him out to sea. He had to be rescued by lifeguards and was quite shaken by this near-tragedy.

Before starting their own US tour back at home, Eddie joined Beth Liebling on the road for a six-week tour by her band Hovercraft, supported by the pre-punkster Dave Watt, on some of whose solo albums Eddie had played. Eddie thoroughly enjoyed being involved in a touring party without the focus being entirely on him. Wearing a sixties wig and big dark shades, he occasionally took to the drum stool of Hovercraft (normally occupied by former Pearl Jam man Dave Krusen) for a whole set. However, many of the gigs came to be swelled by Pearl Jam fans hoping to catch a glimpse of their idol in a small club, so after a few dates Eddie reduced the amount of time spent on stage, but continued to follow the tour around.

His own somewhat larger national tour, the band's first in over a year since Cobain's suicide, was scheduled to start on 16 June in Idaho. The band were undeterred by the prospect of touring without Ticketmaster. Using the much smaller, new agency Entertainment Network, or ETM, they began organising the tour on their own terms. Tickets would cost $18 before a service charge, which would average around just $2. T-shirts were sold for an unusually low $18. Small and unusual venues were chosen and the band announced their intention to play surprise, fan club only gigs at short notice. They also refused to sell limited view seats, and bought satellite time to broadcast one of their shows live on a non-exclusive radio signal.

'Their service [ETM's] is so much better [than Ticketmaster's],' Curtis claimed in *Spin*. 'You don't have to have a credit card to order by phone. You don't have to have advertising on the ticket. We realised that we couldn't put together a safe, efficient tour without using existing venues. In order to do that, we would have to use non-Ticketmaster venues, which means open fields where we install fences, security, amenities . . . It was a logistics thing. It's possible to do a tour without Ticketmaster, but it's an incredible pain in the ass.'

His caution proved to be well-founded – from the outset the tour was bedevilled with logistical and personnel problems, with

Eddie at the centre. Indeed, problems arose before they even set out, with the San Diego Sheriff's Department having two shows scheduled for the Del Mar Fairgrounds moved to a Ticketmaster-controlled venue, the Sports Arena, on safety grounds. Once the tour started, matters got no better. The opening show in Boise, Idaho had to be switched to Casper, Wyoming after yet more ticketing disputes, this time with Boise State University. The second date at Wolf Mountain Amphitheater, in Salt Lake City, was cancelled due to torrential rain and hail. After ten days on the road, Pearl Jam had completed only four gigs.

'It's possible to do a tour without Ticketmaster, but it's an incredible pain in the ass.' *Kelly Curtis*

Eddie took each cancellation personally. After all, just before the tour started he had said, 'If it's not fun this time, then it can't be,' and had gone on, 'I really want people to know about that it's not gonna be this big thing. It's gonna be about music.' With his hopes already dashed, Eddie was in a foul mood by the time the band arrived on the West Coast. There were rumours that he was mentally unwell, and while these were unsubstantiated, it was clear that the recent battles were taking their toll. Things came to a head at the Golden Gate Park on 24 June. Initially everything went well – despite fears that the smaller agency would not handle the expected crowds, the queues moved swiftly and safely and there were very few scalpers, put off by the bar-code swipes and security. Signs that Pearl Jam were still furiously anti-mainstream were indicated by the poster announcing 'Pearl Jam – Sponsored by No One.' However, the atmosphere backstage was strained as Eddie had agreed to allow news photographers in to the concert, but then at the last minute had changed his mind and banned them from the remainder of the tour. The anger among the press pack led to threats that they would boycott the dates altogether.

When Pearl Jam took to the stage, they started strongly, but Eddie seemed unsettled and looked rather grey, his voice breaking unevenly – he even messed up 'Corduroy' completely. Then, without any warning after just seven songs, he walked up to the microphone and said, 'I want to tell you something from my heart. This has been the worst 24 hours of my life. Last night I was puking and shitting – I'm all fucked up. But I think Neil Young's here . . .' and with that, he walked offstage, leaving a stunned crowd and band behind. They had played just 26 minutes. It later transpired that Eddie had been to hospital that morning with stomach flu, and his ailments might have been worsened by the consumption of a room-service tuna-fish sandwich that he claimed later was rancid. The night before he had been invited to a jazz club, but had felt so ill he stayed in reading a copy of *Zlata's Diary: A Child's Life In Sarajevo*, whose thirteen-year-old author he was due to meet at the show the next day. By 5am, after not sleeping at all, Eddie checked into a downtown hospital where he stayed for treatment until 9am. Quite clearly on his arm on stage was a small plaster where he had given a blood sample.

The audience did not take this development well and over half started to leave the arena there and then. Almost immediately the remaining people started abusing the band, one fan reportedly shouting, 'That's gay! I paid $25 for this. He's a fucking asshole. Unbelievable!' When Neil Young did indeed take to the stage about twenty minutes later, bedecked in a tie-dyed Harley Davidson T-shirt, to jam along with the rest of Pearl Jam for the remainder of the show, the crowd's disgust was barely containable, with one fan screaming, 'Hey, this guy's huge in Denver. Neil Young?! Why don't we start listening to Sinatra?'

'We'll try to come back at the end of the tour but, you know, oh well . . .' *Jeff Ament*

The material was well played and the audience politely applauded, but there was no escaping the huge disappointment. Encouraged by Young's occasional tease of 'Let's go see if we can wake up Eddie', everyone figured Eddie would return at some point. He didn't. According to local newspapers, by this time Eddie was already back in his hotel room in bed. After two and a half hours, Young broke the news to the disbelieving crowd, after which Ament offered them some sparse relief, saying, 'We'll try to come back at the end of the tour but, you know, oh well . . .'

Fortunately, the crowd did not riot, as some had feared, even though they had waited seven hours in 100-degree heat with hour-long queues for water. A wave of disappointed resignation swept over them, but there was only a handful of boos. Then, with a stunning lack of tact, a spokesman for the band took the microphone and scolded the crowd for booing, saying they should be grateful for Pearl Jam and that events could not have been helped: 'Pearl Jam does a lot for their fans, you should respect them,' he said. As one magazine put it, 'Fans who called San Francisco radio shows over the next few days to voice their disappointment almost always cited that speech as the exact moment when the band lost them for good.' Some listeners asked the radio never to play Pearl Jam again. The *Austin American-Statesman* angrily wrote: 'For a group that bellows so incessantly in favour of its fans, Pearl Jam sure left a whole bunch of them out in the cold, including the 25,000 people who went through a lot of trouble to get tickets. Pearl Jam's reputation has been damaged, the band's mystique punctured.' The next day, Pearl Jam cancelled the remainder of their fifteen-date tour, blaming 'the business problems and controversies surrounding the band's attempt to schedule an alternative tour'. On the streets of San Francisco, flyers blew across the road saying, 'Pissed off about Pearl Jam? Call this number.' One local radio station christened them 'Pearl Scam'.

• • •

Without explanation, two days after this nadir, Pearl Jam announced that the tour was back on, with re-scheduled dates for many of the cancelled shows. In the aftermath of the debacle, Eddie's feelings were confused: 'I think we all agreed that it had gotten insane, that it was no longer about the music', but soon after, he said, 'Two days later we were calling each other on the phone, there were songs that I was really excited about playing, that everyone was excited about playing.' Ament was still hurt by how harsh the fans had been, telling *Spin*: 'It was amazing to me how unsympathetic some people were to the situation. Neil happened to be there . . . he dragged us back out there. We had our heads down, we were like, "Oh my God, this is the worst fucking day."'

So, the band regrouped, talked for over four hours and agreed to continue. The official explanation came in the form of a statement which said, 'The pressures of a full-scale tour simply took the joy out of making music . . . those pressures would ultimately destroy the band if not dealt with.'

'This is insane. We've got to stop.' *Pearl Jam*

Ironically, the debacle was to pull Pearl Jam closer together: 'That was the day we acted as a band,' Gossard told the *Los Angeles Times*. 'In the past, we had kind of allowed Eddie to steer the ship in some ways, and it's still that way. You want him to feel good about the situation, because when he's feeling good about it, it makes the whole thing work. But that day you could see he was totally sick but still trying to push himself. When we saw what was happening, the band finally said, "This is insane. We've got to stop." We couldn't let him feel like he's got to tour because we're expecting it from him. It was a new beginning.'

Their concern for their singer worked – with amazing swiftness, Eddie soon seemed totally in control again: 'I learned to . . . what's that martial arts phrase? Jeet Kune Do, you know, where someone comes at you with a whole bunch of energy and you just use that energy to let that thing knock itself down. Don't get in there and try to wrestle those things that are so much bigger than you; just divert that whole energy and let that thing trip over itself.' However, once the handful of re-scheduled gigs had been completed, incident-free, within a few weeks, the band's touring of North America was over for 1995. For a group that had sold over 20 million records since 1990, that was hardly sufficient to satisfy the huge demand for live shows. The fans' disgruntled complaints did not go away . . .

• • •

Pearl Jam's association with Neil Young had grown increasingly close since they played at his Bridge Street Benefit in 1992. The logical conclusion of this growing friendship and mutual professional respect was the release in July 1995 of a collaboration album, *Mirrorball*. Many of these songs had been debuted at the ill-fated Golden Gate Park gig. Recorded at Bad Animals Studios, with Brendan O'Brien again at the helm, eleven songs were put down in several intense all-night sessions. Acting largely as Young's backing band for much of the record, Pearl Jam worked on material that the old Crazy Horse had written, fully prepared to defer to his experience and wisdom. The result was effectively a new Neil Young album with a younger Crazy Horse backing him, although Eddie did put his impressive voice to service on the tracks 'Truth Be Known' and 'Peace And Love'. However, despite the album's Top Five success on both sides of the Atlantic, many detractors saw this as further evidence of Pearl Jam's being a part of the mainstream, forming a mutual admiration society with Young.

Eddie was as much inspired by Young's personality as by the music they made together: 'I'm happy to finally have an adult in my life that leads by example, that actually is . . . I've had some crazy adults in my life and it's about time I got one that inspires me.' Ament agreed that the whole project was just the kind of creative fillip the beleaguered band needed: 'Very, very quiet leadership like all the way around. Probably the most inspiring thing that we've ever been involved in, in terms of like just watching every night and not really even talking about it. Just kind of taking it in.' Gossard also drew strength from some live performances they shared with Young and his band, particularly in light of Pearl Jam's own recent difficulties: [They] stay together and work it out. And there's going to be someone who is gonna knock you right on your ass if you're not working it out. I feel like the band finally is a family right now, and that we're in it for the long haul, and that there's nothing we can't work out in terms of being able to play music together. The bottom line is that when we all plug in, Eddie can make us dance and play like little molecules bouncing off the wall. And, for whatever reason, we can make him feel like singing.'

After the release of *Mirrorball* and despite the problematic album tour, Pearl Jam closed 1995 in a stronger sales position than ever before. *Vitalogy* had sold massively, and their previous two albums were still selling extremely well (*Ten* was now past nine million, with *Vs* on six million, leaving *Vitalogy* trying to catch up with a mere five million).

CHAPTER THIRTEEN

STEPPING OUTSIDE THE FRAMEWORK

'The whole point is that we're making music, we're actually feeling something. And people can sense that.'

Eddie

Aafter a lengthy sabbatical during which almost no sight or sound was perceived from them, Pearl Jam returned to the fray in late August 1996 with their fourth album, entitled *No Code*. Having taken on the ticketing business, shunned MTV and generally picked a fight with almost every established interest in the music business, there was really only one area left for Pearl Jam to shock with – their music. *No Code* certainly did that; it was their most diverse, experimental record yet, not so much a change in direction as a veritable U-turn. Brave, possibly suicidal. It was also brilliant.

Shortly after the end of the *Vitalogy* tour, Pearl Jam quietly slipped into NYC Recording Studio and began laying down scraps of material for the new record. Coming off the back of the tour, however fraught with difficulty, meant the band were still very tight, and the recording was consequently very swift and highly productive. Such was the low profile that the band were keeping that the rumour mill went into overdrive to compensate, with magazines that had been starved of Pearl Jam interviews for months devoting whole pages to a meaningless snippet of a story about Eddie playing some sample tracks to Epic executives.

In the studio, Pearl Jam were a band undergoing a re-birth, at the centre of which was Jack Irons. Eddie had originally said Irons 'saved the band', and his words were borne out by this new project. Irons kept the band's momentum going, as Gossard told *Musician* magazine: 'Coming into this album was the most significant time in the last three years, in the sense that everything was up in the air. If we didn't find a drummer that everyone felt good about, it would have been difficult to keep moving forward. Jack's just a very generous and wise drummer. He concentrates on the groove of a song, and that allows everybody's heart to have a place to sit, and yet be part of the whole. He's very conscious of what everybody's playing. He's working to balance out all the elements of the band.' Eddie agreed, saying in *Spin*: 'This should have been the band from the beginning, it's a new relationship, one of life's adjustments.' For his own part, Irons was somewhat more laid back, saying, 'The whole point is that we're making music, we're actually feeling something. And people can sense that.'

Irons's flexibility was perfectly welcome in a situation where Pearl Jam seemed to ignore almost everything they had done previously. The sign of intent came with the very first track, the quiet confessional 'Sometimes' which opened the album with an almost New Age gentleness, Eddie hushing over a sparse and hypnotic lilt. Next up was the Who-like 'Hail Hail' which was more typically Pearl Jam, although even this was noticeably different, with Stone Gossard debuting on strangely warbled vocals. Irons's calculated approach could be especially seen on one of the best tracks, the Eastern-influenced 'Who You Are', of which McCready said, 'When I first heard that song, I was totally blown away by it, I thought it was the best song we had ever done.' For this track, which many pundits claimed referred to Eddie's work with the late Pakistani vocalist Nusrat Fateh Ali Khan (Eddie had recently worked with him on two songs for the soundtrack to the Tim Robbins film *Dead Man Walking)*, Irons took a Max Roach drum solo he said he'd 'been playing since I was eight. I heard it at a drum shop when I was a little kid.' His tumbling tom-tom made the track.

'Coming into this album was the most significant time in the last three years.' *Stone Gossard*

'In My Tree' was in many ways more reminiscent of early eighties U2 than Pearl Jam, sounding like stadium rock but with a quiet restraint. Again Eddie's famously powerful vocals were slightly less pained, more controlled than hitherto. Irons's drum circles that accompanied the crescendo climax brought U2's Larry Mullen Jr instantly to mind. 'Smile', was more like Neil Young and

Crazy Horse, an influence that was found in various parts of the album, understandably in respect of the band's recent collaborations. Throughout, the album was characterised by change: one minute Pearl Jam were funky, the next folk, they mixed acoustic with rock, spoken word with wailing screamed vocals – anything seemed to be acceptable.

'I think it was probably the funniest record that we've ever made together.' *Stone Gossard*

In the country and western-style 'Off He Goes' it seemed Eddie was at last confronting the persona he had been given by the media, talking of a man, his face frowning and tense, in scruffy clothes, pursuing hopeless dreams. Shortly after, an album highlight, the manic and quirky 'Lukin' smashed in at just 60 seconds, and along with the crunching 'Smile', 'Mankind', and the Lemmy-like 'Hail, Hail' kept up Pearl Jam's resident quota of hard-hitting rockers. One of these tunes, 'Mankind', was a tribute to the Bacchanal, the underground club in Seattle where so many great bands had been given their first break.

Gossard told listeners to KISW 99.9 FM Radio in Seattle how the band were pleased with the music, and doubly pleased with what their new-found communicative nature meant for their future: 'We're all totally happy with the way it turned out, I mean we were as happy as we've ever been making records. I think it was probably the funniest record that we've ever made together which was a really nice thing as far as like all of us kind of being in the studio all the time and really enjoying each other. And, I don't know, it's kind of a good time right know for us on a personal relationship level.' He also said, 'We're more confident now about the band's longevity and our relationships with each other. We may take breaks and do other things, but we feel we'll ultimately have Pearl Jam as a family. It's really comforting for me and Jeff, at least, that after twelve years we finally feel we've reached a place where we can be more honest, real and loving with each other. And we're finally in a band that we know is good, and deserves the credit.' Also, for the first time he related to much of what Eddie was singing: 'Except for a few moments on the first record, a lot of times Eddie's lyrics were just stories to me. I knew he was a great writer and there was a lot passion behind the lyrics, but I didn't always relate to them. On this record, it's like my own thoughts are in the songs. In some ways, it's like the band's story. It's about growing up.'

The press, startled and impressed by the new direction Pearl Jam seemed to be heading in, agreed. Take this review from the otherwise recalcitrant *Rolling Stone*: 'If anything, Pearl Jam are vigilant and hopeful – if sometimes inconsistent – pragmatists. They're empowered by platinum and unembarrassed by their sense of mission, willing to risk tripping over their own hard line to make a vital point. And they're not so self-righteous as to deny that, yes, success has its privileges. For example, if you can't put out a glorious, guiltless, mad blend of tunes and weird tangents like *No Code* when you're at the top, what's the point of swimming through all the sewage to get there.' David Fricke also noted that, as Jimi Hendrix once said, if you can't re-invent yourself in rock 'n' roll, 'There ain't no life nowhere.' The same magazine also said of the album, '*No Code* doesn't quite have the concentrated, brawling force of *Vs* or the focused sweep of *Vitalogy*. The album is certainly a big awkward leap from the burnished, arena-ripe sheen of *Ten*. But in its own brash, off-center way, *No Code* is a real gas – charged with pungent declaration and heaving guitars; warm and even a little wry in low throttle; elastic in its attack and intimate in its tension. It is the kind of impulsive, quixotic, provocative ruckus that has become rare in a modern rock mainstream, largely distinguished by weary fatalism and anxiety over quick career burn-out. As a record, as a declaration of honour, *No Code* basically means no rule books, no limits and, above all, no fear.'

It might seem easy to be fearless when sitting on the royalties of three multi-million selling albums, and all the critical acclaim and popular idolisation that goes with that, but this last comment really sums up the ethos of *No Code* and why Pearl Jam were brave to make it. Even after so many public *faux pas*, the cancelled gigs, the ticket difficulties and so on, Pearl Jam were still asking their fans, almost recklessly challenging them, to try new sounds and forget their previous favourites. For a band at the pinnacle of their apparent 'cock-rock' and 'corporate grunge' career, this was a daredevil, experimental and ultimately admirable step. But it also

*Eddie regularly fuels himself from a bottle
of wine when performing.*

seemed that they had to take this step in order to survive; as Eddie succinctly put it, 'Making *No Code* was all about gaining perspective.'

However, the band were dealt a harsh lesson in commercial perspective when the album was released. Although *No Code* hit the Number 1 spot in America in its first week, it sold only 367,000 copies, huge by most people's standards but a definite setback for Pearl Jam. What's more, after only two months in the chart the record dropped out of the Top Twenty listings, compared to *Ten* which was in the Top 100 for 105 weeks. Moreover, the single 'Who You Are' was deliberately chosen as being non-radio friendly and proved to be triumphantly so, with many stations hardly playing it at all. Undeterred, perhaps even encouraged, and with a small US tour at exclusively non-Ticketmaster venues, followed by a nineteen-date European tour, Pearl Jam were straining at the leash to get out and play their dramatically diverse new material. With claims that their continually anti-commercial approach (no new videos and still no interviews) would be their own destruction loudly ringing in their ears, they hit the road eagerly. Manager Kelly Curtis reflected the upbeat mood in the camp when he said, 'The band is very excited to get back out in front of the fans and play some shows. We've got some new music. It's going to be a blast.'

With a disappointing solitary show on the West Coast, and with no show at all in Los Angeles, most Pearl Jam fans in California and Oregon had to travel to Seattle for a public concert. (The tour was predominantly based on the East Coast.) Things kicked off with a typical low-key fan-club only gig on 14 September, at the Showbox Theatre in the same city, where the band demanded that no executives, press or PR be allowed. As a result, they took to the stage in front of 800 faithful fans for a show which proved at least that much of even the least accessible *No Code* material had special life breathed into it in live performance. Tracks like 'Present Tense', 'In My Tree' and 'Sometimes', took on a new energy, although the fragile ballad 'Sometimes' nevertheless proved to be a muted opener, but conversely the more traditional Pearl Jam rock anthem of 'Hail, Hail' seemed a little subdued. Eddie was noticeably more static, and Ament was similarly rooted to the spot, with no sign of his famous scissor kicks and flying jumps. A few fans cast worried glances at each other as the band seemed to be increasingly disinterested, a concern confirmed when Eddie said, 'This is the part of the show we call the human jukebox,' before they played a selection of crowd-pleasers from their previous three albums. Unsurprisingly, their spirit was missing and despite the successes with some of the new songs, overall the set was disappointing, as Eddie acknowledged at the end when he said, 'Well, this was almost worth leaving the house for.'

Other dates on the tour were not all so quiet, and some people talked of the band regaining the explosive live venom that had been such a crucial part of their early success. However, Eddie was even more vocal than before in between songs, sometimes grumbling endlessly while the crowd watched, bored, waiting for another number. When he arrived in New York, he had obviously gotten wind of the forthcoming *Rolling Stone* article with its portrayal of a comfortable childhood, and he used the gig to set a few matters straight, butting in to the middle of 'Who Are You' to say 'I know who I really am. It's a long story, and it won't fit . . . in a rolling stone.'

The dispute with Ticketmaster was seen by some observers as having sapped their energy. They agreed to perform at one Ticketmaster venue, but only if all the proceeds were donated to charity (tickets for the entire tour were very reasonably priced at between $15 and $22.50, with the dreaded service charge kept to around $2). With only twelve dates across the whole of America, and another labyrinthine telephone system for getting hold of tickets, commentators wondered if the distractions surrounding Eddie had finally eclipsed the music. *Rolling Stone* were far from forgiving: 'It's clear from the pit of moshers down front that this crowd wants nothing more than to rock out to its favourite Pearl Jam oldies, but Vedder seems determined to thwart his fans, draining the show's energy with earnest speeches between songs. "We didn't use a promoter," he announces. "I hate to even mention it, but we do it all ourselves." Soon the music begins to seem little more than a backdrop to Vedder's speechifying, the fans little more than a receptacle for Vedder's polemics.'

The tour only really started to kick into life when the band flew to Europe, with Eastern Europe being particularly receptive (although it was a big money-loser for Pearl Jam). The band loved the privacy afforded to them by the low key music media over there, and their anonymity on the streets during the day was an unexpected bonus. Unfortunately, where the music media have the highest profile, that is, in America and the UK, the knives were out.

In various ways things were looking bleak commercially. First, the music world had undergone a transformation since the heyday of grunge. In Britain, the poppier and more humorous Britpop had swept back the US invasion that grunge had brought, leaving slacker culture obsolete and unfashionable in the face of the rise of Blur, Pulp, and, of course, Oasis. In America, too, the resurgence of lighter pop music had left grunge sounding tired, uninspired and unpopular, as the music world became bored with the often dour Seattle sound.

This was reflected in the relatively poor sales of *No Code*, although it still went platinum after four months, topping over 1.1 million. Pearl Jam had not helped sales with the artwork, insisting their name was not on the cover, instead opting for a collage of random photographs.

The lack of commercial promotion remained a sticking point with the band's detractors and, increasingly, with their fans, who were frustrated by their inability to see their heroes on the television alongside their other favourites. This same problem applied to their tours. Although the band had started their lonely crusade against Ticketmaster in order to benefit their fans, the truncated tours, sometimes obscure venues and often complex ticket systems had actually made life less easy for the kids. Growing tired of waiting for the next Pearl Jam gig, only to find there would not be one for hundreds of miles, fans started to go to see other bands. People said Eddie's obsessions were distancing the band from their fanbase.

This was worsened by Eddie's grumblings about being a rock star, which many felt smacked of decadence and an inflated ego. A good example of this was at the 38th Annual Grammy Awards in February 1997, when Pearl Jam scooped the Best Hard Rock Performance Award. Rather than protest by staying away altogether, Eddie turned up for his first television appearance in two years in an expensive looking leather coat and shades, and mumbled, 'This doesn't mean anything' on being given the award. No word for the fans who had waited so patiently for this moment. Nothing. Although they knew he disliked awards ceremonies, calling them inherently ludicrous by setting up bands against one another, this did little to satiate their hunger or appease

Eddie took to delivering earnest speeches during the tour to promote No Code.

their frustrations.

The contentious *Rolling Stone* article quoted one so-called 'Epic staffer' as saying, 'It's all caught up to them. No band is bigger than the system, and consumers are punishing them. Pearl Jam hurt themselves when they don't do things America wants. If you only do twelve shows, you need to do videos to remind the country what you look like'. Timothy White of *Billboard* magazine agreed when he said to *Spin*, 'There has to be a basic dialogue between your band and your public. People want an ebb and flow of ideas, and they just don't understand the degree of reticence that has crept up around the band.' The inevitable momentum of all these factors was to weaken Pearl Jam commercially. One unnamed industry veteran was quoted as saying, 'Pearl Jam always said they didn't want to be stars. Well, it looks like they may soon have their wish.' Another executive said, 'I think they are still a very, very important band culturally, but they've got to re-think the way they promote themselves if they want to continue to be one of the big players. The way it is now, they are cutting themselves off from their fans. With some changes, however, they could be as big as ever. It's their choice.' The industry was rife with rumours – were Pearl Jam's days as a multi-platinum-selling band over?

'We're not going to look at the financial end and make decisions based on that.' *Eddie Vedder*

The answer is they very probably were. The band genuinely didn't care. Indeed, they were actively encouraged by the change, none more so than Eddie Vedder. In a rare interview with *Spin*, the band appeared clearly to be far from perturbed by the smaller sales and the public dissatisfaction. After all, money was no longer an object, and hadn't been for some time. Musically, they had progressed hugely with their last album, and their lower profile and smaller tours meant they felt far more in control. Eddie summed up their mood when he said, 'It's great! We can be a little more normal now.'

He was also quite direct about Pearl Jam's motivations for the future: 'We're selfish. We want it to be about the music. We don't really care about any of this stuff. We don't feel we need to justify anything. We know where we're coming from, and then it gets misconstrued, or people don't understand certain things, like why you couldn't play in San Francisco, or why you don't participate with the music channel. You definitely feel like responding to a lot of this stuff, but then you realise that it just kind of goes away. As long as you focus on the music, all that stuff doesn't matter.'

Eddie continued: 'We're not going to look at the financial end and make decisions based on that. If it doesn't feel right, we don't want to do it. I'm kind of proud of that.' He had every right to be. This new franchise was exclusive of the public, and yes, those fans who had put him where he was, at least financially. But at the same time, Pearl Jam had often stood up for fans' issues, despite facing abuse and criticism in return – the Ticketmaster issue, pricing tickets cheaply, making radio broadcasts. As for the repercussions finally catching up with them, Eddie was again startlingly blunt: 'I guess what has happened to us with this record shows that promotion really does matter, just like everybody told us. If you don't operate in that framework, which we don't, it's obvious that you won't sell as many records. And that's fine. We expected this to happen much sooner than it has. To us, it's about choices and lifestyles. Do you want to spend your time on the road and doing promotion, or do you spend your time making music and living your life? At the end of the day, what is most important? To us, I'd like to think it's our music and the quality of our lives.'

Those who realised that healthy bands are not simply those that sell by the million agreed. One insider said, 'What has happened with this record has taken some of the pressure off the band. The whole reluctance to do press and video wasn't some anti-establishment statement. One of the concerns was they didn't want to do anything that would explode their fame even further. Some of that pressure is off now and that makes it liberating. I wouldn't be surprised to see them do a few more things, even a video at some point.' In the meantime, small tours of no more than 30 or so dates are planned, although no mention of a video has been made by the band camp. 'I think touring is always going to be a compromise,' Ament told the *Los Angeles Times*. 'Eddie and Jack are both married and they don't like to tour a lot, while some of us would probably like to tour more. I can go either way.'

CHAPTER FOURTEEN

THE INVOLUNTARY RECLUSE

'There's no school to go to for some of the weird shit that happens.'
Eddie

Although he was the last man to join the original line-up back in 1990, Eddie has long since been acknowledged by his colleagues as the spiritual leader of the group. Obviously on stage he takes the lead, but his keenness for benefit shows, the album artwork, his reluctance to be interviewed and his involvement in the managerial side of the band have fuelled rumours that the rest of the band are cowed by his power drive: 'Other band members look to him to make decisions,' a confidential source at the band's label, Epic, told *Rolling Stone*. 'Everybody gets input, but Eddie leads the way.' Another Epic staffer was more direct, saying Eddie was a 'control freak' and spoke of everyone having to 'walk on eggshells'.

Amidst rumours of internal conflicts, some people have suggested that his four band colleagues live in fear of either being sacked or of Eddie leaving, and that the dismissal of Abbruzzese (who was recognised as annoying Eddie, although Gossard did the firing) sent a message of discipline to the rest of the remaining members. All this suggests that Pearl Jam rest on a fragile foundation, as might be substantiated by the number of side projects these individual members pursue.

In fact, Pearl Jam's five members have always pursued other projects on their own. Perhaps the most notable of these has been Stone Gossard's own record label, Loosegroove Records. Based in Seattle (where else?) Loosegroove had satisfied Gossard's wish to help out struggling bands in their early days. In this fashion, he has released records by such diverse acts as Weapon of Choice, Malfunkshun (which used to feature Mother Love Bone singer Andrew Wood), hip hop band Pros and Concepts, Devilhead, and

Critters Buggin' (which features former Pearl Jam drummer Matt Chamberlain). Another act that Loosegroove release is Brad, which is the band that features Gossard himself, along with Satchel's Sean Smith.

Ament formed the pseudo-eastern Three Fish. McCready started off with the brooding Mad Season (alongside Alice In Chains' Layne Staley and Martin Barrett from Screaming Trees, whose Mark Lanegan also helped out) but has since played in a myriad of side projects, including work with his jazz-based Tuatura, and the rockier Minus Five. Even Eddie himself has dabbled outside the band, with his soundtrack work with Nusrat Fateh Ali Khan and some spoken-word contributions to a tribute album to Jack Kerouac. Before he departed, Dave Abbruzzese had played drums on Course Of Empire's *God's Jig*.

'Hopefully, people will continue to extend me the benefit of the doubt. If not . . . well, I've gotten a lot, and I appreciate it all.' *Eddie Vedder*

In more contented times, these side projects were seen as mere diversions from the main cause, but with the decline in the band's popularity, they were being cited as evidence that the other members of the band were arranging their post-Pearl Jam careers already. Eddie himself did not deny he had considered the possibilities of calling it a day when he told *Spin*, 'Hopefully, people will continue to extend me the benefit of the doubt. If not . . . well, I've gotten a lot, and I appreciate it all. But I could also see myself trading it all in.'

The band, of course, deny this is in their minds. Gossard admits he has allowed Eddie to encroach into songwriting more and more, but with reason: 'If it had remained always my band,' he told *Musician* magazine, 'my natural tendency would have been to get more complex and arrange things more and more. That wouldn't necessarily be good for Eddie, or anyone else in the band. Of course, I enjoy being self-indulgent. And I look forward to the time when I can become more indulgent with my songwriting. But this band is a family, and it's a process that we have to grow with together. There's no getting around the fact that Eddie is the man. As far as emotional and spiritual energy goes, he is the leader of this band. But Eddie does not make all the decisions. Eddie can listen to reason; Eddie can be swayed or talked in or out of certain things. Eddie allows other people to lead in this band and to have certain roles that are very fundamental to the decision-making process. Eddie is a natural leader. Jeff and I have been very much in control of previous bands we've worked in. But the way Eddie grew into being the leader of this band was the most gradual, slow and respectful process that I've ever been involved in. That's not to say Eddie's never done anything malicious. But he never grabbed power for power's sake. His position was gained only because he has that energy, and that's naturally where he ended up.'

When *Rolling Stone* asked Kelly Curtis in 1994 if Eddie might leave the band, he replied, 'I believe he thinks about that every day.' Another Epic Records source told the magazine, 'I was really pushing Eddie to do something he didn't want to do, I was told: "Just don't push him too far, or he'll just go away."' Apparently, that's a possibility that no one associated with Pearl Jam wants to contemplate . . .

• • •

So where did Eddie Vedder stand, and what was his mind-set after *No Code*? In previous interviews, it was clear that the vagaries of fame were still something he could not always handle: 'I feel like, you know, you go out of your way, but everyone is so fucking cynical,' he told *Spin*, 'that you can't even do something good without someone thinking that you've got another play on it. No one seems to know how to deal with honesty anymore. They see someone being honest and they think there's got to be a hidden agenda there. And it's really fucking it up for some of us who are coming clean. I'm just totally vulnerable. I'm way too fucking soft for this whole business, this whole trip. I don't have any shell.' While the other four members are regularly spotted on the Seattle music scene, sightings of Eddie are rare. The circle of friends that he trusts is small and he spends most of his time cocooned in his new, large house in a middle-class area of West Seattle, on a tree-lined street overlooking Puget Sound. For many years, he still drove the same Toyota truck that he owned when he was working at the gas station, but then decided, 'I don't need to do things like that to remind me of who I am. But maybe it's good that other people see those things and maybe it sends them a message, that I still am the same person.'

One of the reasons for this increased withdrawal was the attentions of an alleged stalker, who apparently claimed his girlfriend's obsession with Eddie led to the break-up of their relationship, and vowed to exact his revenge on the singer. Eddie has also had many death threats and was forced, against his will, to employ 24-hour security guards at his home, complete with ferocious dogs. A short-wave radio hack was tapping into his cordless phone conversations and fans hid outside his house waiting for glimpses. This entrenchment of his own home saddened Eddie greatly: 'What's really sad about the whole thing is that Beth and I are the kind of people who'd love to ask some kid, some fan, into our house, you know, sit them down and play them records from our jukebox, that kind of thing, but we just can't do that now.'

'. . .maybe it's good that other people see those things and maybe it sends them a message, that I still am the same person'. *Eddie Vedder*

Despite all his efforts to the contrary, Eddie has become the archetypal reclusive rock star. The irony is that his efforts to win better deals for the fans, with cheaper tickets and fewer interviews and videos, have only increased the hunger for a piece of him. By withdrawing from the game, he has effectively placed himself at the most frenzied, bizarre centre of it all. Now obsessive fans get excited when they discover what flavour of pizza Eddie has delivered every week, while the security men have to thoroughly search the pizza delivery man before he goes in. Eddie has said that he has even considered building a huge castle in which to lock himself away, but dismissed the idea as too absurd – 'What am I going to do to escape this kind of thing? I'm a target.' Although he claims to do everyday things, like laundry and writing, Eddie's life is no longer based on normality.

'I don't feel like people relate to me as a normal human.'

Eddie Vedder

Eddie himself noticed this as far back as 1994, when he told *Spin,* 'I don't think anyone can understand what it's like. It's just so strange, it just seems like there are all these people out there that would love to be my friend or something, yet I don't really have any. Because I don't know who to relate to. I don't know how people relate to me. I don't feel like people relate to me as a normal human.'

CHAPTER FIFTEEN

INTO THE WILD

'We've learned how to balance everything out now in terms of how much you live in the press world and how much time you live making music with your friends.'

Stone

In late 1997, as the individual members of Pearl Jam's involvement with a host of side-projects fuelled rumours of an imminent split, the band themselves were deep into sessions for their next album at Stone Gossard's Studio Litho in Seattle.

The new album, again produced by Brendan O'Brien at the downtown Bad Animal Studios, was recorded with speed and enthusiasm by the revitalised group. Titled *Yield*, the record was released on 2 February 1998, preceded by the single 'Given To Fly' on 19 January.

Yield marked a return to a harder style: *Rolling Stone* described it as 'the rawest stuff they've done since *Vs.*'. The tracks were looser and funkier than the Pearl Jam of old, featuring the dense guitar sound of grunge, but not smothered by it. On ballad-tempo songs like 'Low Light' and 'In Hiding', Eddie stretched his voice to its fullest degree. 'Given To Fly' paid tribute to Pearl Jam's 1970s FM rock roots, while Eddie even managed emotional full-on love songs with 'Faithful' and the heartfelt 'Wishlist'. More sombre, 'Low Light' was almost a devotional hymn, while 'Pilate' namechecked the legendary Roman governor who metaphorically washed his hands of Christ.

All members of the band contributed to the songwriting process and for the first time the lyrics were not exclusively written by Eddie. 'When we were making *No Code*,' recalled Jeff Ament, 'Ed said, "It would be great if everyone brought in more complete songs and ideas next time." And everybody stepped up to the challenge.

'Now we were all able to work off each other's demos and begin to hammer something out after twenty minutes or so. It was much easier to approach these songs as "our", as opposed to "my", song.'

Ament's contributions to the album's more philosophical songs – 'Do The Evolution' and 'Push Me, Pull Me' – were also born of a new approach to life: 'I spent a lot of time in the woods or in the mountains, and I started to realise I'm not as important as I thought I was when I was 28.'

Further evidence of this lighter atmosphere came with Pearl Jam's decision to issue a studio-based video for 'Given To Fly'. Cynics suggested this belated embracing of MTV had much to do with the relatively declining sales of the band's last two albums, *Vitalogy* and *No Code*. Mike McCready also confirmed that the Ticketmaster battle was being wound down to the extent where it would no longer distract from the band's music. 'We might actually do some shows with them in certain cities,' he conceded, 'because you can't really deal without them in places like Chicago and Philadelphia.' But it was of strictly secondary importance this time around. As manager Kelly Curtis acknowledged, 'I think they're over the hump and back to being a band again.'

After four November '97 warm-up dates supporting the Rolling Stones at Oakland Stadium, CA, the band's first promotional world tour in over four years began at the Maui Arts and Cultural Centre in Hawaii. 'I just wanted tonight to be perfect,' Eddie told the audience on opening night. 'I've been waiting a long, long time.'

Although the band had reluctantly conceded that Ticketmaster's stranglehold over concert venues and ticketing made it impractical to boycott the sales and distribution company and put together an accessible tour, Pearl Jam's radical, zealous edge endured. At the Hawaiian opening night, some protesters passed a banner to the band that read, 'SAVE MAALAEA' – a reference to a traditional site being made over by developers into a new harbour. They earned Eddie's full vocal support. 'Don't stop there,' he addressed the protesters from on stage. 'Keep going. Burn some bulldozers or something. And tell 'em I told you to.'

Pearl Jam's 1998 world tour was a celebration for all concerned. Even the intense Eddie was seen to crack a smile to the audience once in a while. 'Living on the road is kind of like an acquired skill,' said Stone Gossard, 'and if you haven't used that skill in a while it begins to deteriorate. We've had to get our road legs back in working condition.'

'For all Eddie Vedder's sincerity, he was always auditioning too hard for the Troubled Childhood All-Stars,' opined *Rolling Stone* in their review of *Yield*. 'Like the rest of the band, he seemed . . . as though he was afraid no one would take him seriously if he got caught having fun.' In public, however, Eddie appeared in great spirits. Even Mike admitted, 'I used to be afraid of him and not want to confront him on things. I felt I was always walking on eggshells around him. Now I just feel more confident and comfortable with myself, and maybe the mutual respect comes out of that.'

On a personal level, this mutual respect also came from the conquering of personal demons. 'I was probably close to being kicked out of the band around the time of *Vitalogy*,' Mike admitted. 'I was pretty fucked up. When we were recording that album I was drinking the entire mini-bar, eating Valium and doing all this stupid shit like not showing up for sessions.' With his drinking under control, the guitarist was back to being a fully contributing member of a fully functional unit. Everyone was pulling their weight – although drummer Jack Irons, who Mike praised as 'a big spiritual influence' for his personal role as band mediator, was starting to exhibit problems of his own.

As the band re-acclimatised themselves to the road, demand on the US leg of their tour was as high as it ever had been. 'You can usually judge how hot a band is by how quick a show sells out,' one East Coast ticket 'scalper' was quoted by *Hit Parader* magazine, 'and by how high those who missed out on buying tickets will go to get some. The Pearl Jam shows are routinely going two-times over face value.'

While the demand may have provided commercial reassurance to the band's management, the unauthorised profiteering by scalpers gave them another enemy to rail against. 'You want all your fans to get the tickets,' Stone complained. 'Ideally, there would be a way of assuring a certain limited number be given to each customer. But it's virtually impossible to monitor that. We'd love to see it happen, but we haven't figured out a way of doing it yet.'

One other consequence of the *Yield* tour was a line-up change. Early on in the tour, Jack Irons went on a leave of absence reputedly due to depression. 'He was a guy whom everybody had wanted in the band,' confirmed manager Kelly Curtis, 'and initially he really had a great effect on everybody. But he stepped into the PJ world, and it was pretty overwhelming. He wasn't able to continue.'

'We went and did Hawaii and Australia with Jack,' recalled sound engineer Brett Eliason. 'When he came back, Jack wasn't in a position to carry on. He made that decision more or less by himself. He can be a really great drummer but he had difficulty on tour putting out the energy for the length of shows they were doing. I don't know if he thought they'd put things on hold for him.'

'I got a phone call out of the blue, from Mr Ed, Stoney and Kelly,' explained former Soundgarden drummer Matt Cameron. 'I was ambushed. It was really short notice. He called and said, "Hey, what are you doing this summer?"'

'He's not joined the band, he's touring with the band,' insisted one of Matt's spokesmen. But Cameron, of course, had history with Pearl Jam: in the band's early days, he had been the drummer on demo versions of 'Alive', 'Even Flow' and 'Animal'; latterly, he'd beaten the skins for Temple of the Dog, the Seattle rock side-project featuring members of Pearl Jam and Soundgarden. 'End of tour, Eddie said, "Hey, man, you want to join?"' confirmed Matt. 'I said, "Let me think about it." So I said, "I'll do a record, do a tour, if you wouldn't mind me doing it that way." I haven't really joined them long-term.' But with Pearl Jam, it was almost like he was coming home. 'They're kind of in a special league,' he said approvingly. 'They can tour really comfortably but keep it kinda small as well. Punk-rock arena rock is the way they approach it.'

As if to celebrate being back on the road, Pearl Jam found an unlikely camp follower. Superstar basketball player Dennis Rodman had buddied up with Jeff Ament, who used to play basketball on a college team. 'He's definitely living the life of a rock star, way more so than us,' confirmed Jeff. 'I threw a lot of drinks over my shoulder, just kind of pretending I was going along for the ride.' Rodman outstayed his welcome, however, when he drunkenly took to the stage during a 1998 Texas date. 'He would go behind Stone and start strumming on the guitar while Stone was playing,' remembers Soundgarden manager Susan Silver, who witnessed the gig, 'or just walk in front of Stone and talk about how incredible each guy was. They finally got a stool and set him in front of the drum kit, leering at Matt from right in front like, "I don't know you, who are you, show me what you got, prove it."'

Yield would ultimately yield up Pearl Jam's next platinum album, after six months of sales. Following the 23 September 1998 culmination of their 23-date US tour, a spokeswoman for their management announced that Pearl Jam had already begun work on a new 'project' scheduled for international release at the end of November: the band's first ever official live album.

(At the beginning of the previous month, Sony had slapped an injunction on the Best Buy chain stores when they announced plans to issue an unauthorised seventeen-track Pearl Jam live album, *Give Way*, as an accompaniment to the band's home video, *Single Video Theory* – a musical documentary about the making of *Yield*.)

Entitled *Pearl Jam Live On Two Legs*, it was recorded at their 19 September Voters for Choice (pro-abortion rights) benefit concert at the Constitution Hall, Washington, D.C., featuring a selection of tracks from throughout the band's career and a cover of friend and mentor Neil Young's proto-grunge song, 'Fuckin' Up'.

The career renaissance that began with *Yield* continued well into the summer of 1999, when Pearl Jam scored their biggest ever hit single in the form of 'Last Kiss', which was remarkable on two counts. Firstly, because it achieved maximum nationwide airplay with little advertising, no radio promotion and no MTV video. 'It's not their style to hire a bunch of people to go around and talk about how great Pearl Jam is,' said Kelly Curtis.

More remarkable still, 'Last Kiss' was released purely by default. Originating at a soundcheck at the end of the *Yield* tour, it was a cover version of an early 1960s hit by J. Frank Wilson and the Cavaliers, a 'death rock' ballad in which the lugubrious vocalist croons about his dead lover. 'Brett [Eliason] recorded it later,' confirmed Stone, 'we spent $1,500 mixing the single at home, and it was our biggest song ever. The same performance that was at soundcheck. Just us trying to sound like a fifties song and sounding half-assed. Ed's interpretation is sentimental and beautiful, and it's not ironic, or clever, or sarcastic.'

Pearl Jam released the song strictly as a festive freebie for the Ten Club, their official fan organisation. 'We're not doing anything with the Ten Club that's completely groundbreaking but it doesn't ever take a back seat,' confirmed club manager, Tim Bierman. 'The Christmas single, that's their present back to their fans and it's always been two unreleased songs on a 45 with original artwork.'

Later fan-club gems would include a double A-side recorded at the band's tenth anniversary show at the MGM Grand Hotel, Las Vegas, on 22 October 2000, covering Elvis' classic 'Can't Help Falling In Love', the Mother Love Bone song 'Crown Of Thorns' – sung in its original form by Eddie's late predecessor, Andrew Wood, on the soundtrack to the Cameron Crowe film *Singles* – and the Ramones' minimalist 'I Just Want To Have Something To Do'.

As radio DJs acquired their own copies of 'Last Kiss', the officially unreleased record began to pick up airplay – until its popularity compelled Pearl Jam to make it an official single release. 'There was this pressure to release it commercially,' recalls Kelly. 'We came up with the idea that you can release it, but you've got to give all the money away.' All band royalties were donated to a relief fund for victims of the Kosovan War.

'You didn't know what the marketplace was and you didn't know how to digest any of that,' Eddie recalls with hindsight. 'It just reaffirmed the fact that you don't have to think about it and that a soundcheck record can do well.'

'That's the way it's supposed to be done,' praised a spokesperson at Sony, parent company of Epic. 'No smoke and mirrors. People just like the song.' Ultimately, 'Last Kiss' reached Number 2 on the *Billboard* Hot 100 chart, and sold half a million copies.

And the momentum kept on rolling. May 2000 saw the release of the next Pearl Jam album, *Binaural*. Named after the way in which sound is perceived simultaneously by both ears, it was produced by Tchad Blake of the Laughing Playboys, whose production track record included blues veteran Bonnie Raitt, and mixed by former producer Brendan O'Brien. 'We'd done four records together, five counting the Neil Young one,' confirmed O'Brien, with no trace of bitterness. 'For whatever reason, they decided to make a record on their own. It was time for that. There was no weirdness. Mike called me up; he was so sweet about it. Classic Mike McCready. "Are you OK? Are you alright?" But when they finished it, I guess they didn't really like the way it sounded. I don't really know. They called me up and said, "Can you help us out?"'

As with *Yield*, the new album was a true collaborative effort. 'They were really adamant about me bringing in songs for *Binaural*,' confirmed Matt Cameron. 'I brought four or five, and Ed really liked the one that became "Evacuation", wanted to write lyrics for it . . . had a real clear idea of what he wanted the song to be.'

Once again, however, Mike was labouring under the emotional and substance abuse problems that had previously dogged him. 'I was going through some personal problems. It was my own stuff I was dealing with,' he confirms. 'That was a tough time. I was out of it. That was due, at the time, I was taking prescription drugs. I got caught up in it, because of my pain.' To his credit, none of it proved detrimental to the album, and Eddie continued to express fraternal concern: 'I hope he knows that at least with the four of us and the people we work with too that he's got solid ground. And that people love him . . .'

Binaural also featured the band's hit single 'Nothing As It Seems', which had first been performed live at one of Neil Young's Bridge School benefit concerts, the previous October. The rest of the album ran the gamut of styles: from Pearl Jam's trademark 1990s hard rock, through speedy post-punk, downbeat folk-style ballads and modern psychedelia.

Eddie's vocals were at their most earthily real and expressive. He howled his protest at the World Trade Organisation and the way it perpetuates Third World poverty in 'Grievance', optimistically insisted it was 'time to take heed and change direction' in the fidgety 'Evacuation', and even performed an anti-materialist ballad, 'Soon Forget', to nothing but a sparse ukulele backing (or a 'grunge-ulele', according to drummer Cameron). 'I'm writing on ukulele a lot,' confirmed old-fashioned boy Eddie. 'It's an interesting instrument, 'cause it's four strings, and the fewer the strings, the more melody, I'm finding. And it's also about the smallest instrument you can play. So I'm just shrinking.'

Binaural was followed, in the next month, by Pearl Jam's most audacious project yet. About to embark on a 28-date European tour to promote the album, the band determined they would beat the bootleggers who traditionally recorded their gigs for pirate albums by producing their *own*. In fact, they planned to release a separate live album for every one of those 28 performances. 'It's been disheartening to hear about fans paying anything up to $50 for poor-quality bootlegs,' explained Kelly. 'Our hope is to provide fans currently buying bootlegs with an alternative.'

This strategy would grant Pearl Jam the distinction of being the only band to have five albums enter the *Billboard* Top 200 simultaneously. 'For God's sake,' joked Mike, 'don't try and listen to all of them. They'll wind up driving you crazy!' The following January, they would continue this policy by issuing a further 23 'official bootlegs' from the American leg of the world tour. A 25-song live DVD, *Touring Band 2000*, would also be issued, culled from fifteen different shows. In the meantime, the number of CDs issued under the collective title *Live In Europe* was whittled down to 25 – due partly to quality control, but also because one fateful performance would be omitted from the running sequence.

During the 1990s, longtime Who fan Eddie Vedder had become a personal friend of his idols. After playing several low-key gigs with Who guitarist and songwriter Pete Townshend, he opened in a solo slot for the Who at one of their comeback shows, a 13 November 1999 benefit for abused children at Chicago's House of Blues. On the 2001 tribute album, *Substitute: The Songs Of The Who*, Pearl Jam would cover Townshend's 1960s beat group ballad 'The Kids Are Alright'. In the summer of 2000, however, it would be Townshend's turn to offer moral support to Eddie – who, along with the rest of Pearl Jam, was devastated by a tragedy, the nature of which the Who were only too familiar with.

On Friday 30 June, 2000, Pearl Jam were performing on the latest leg of their European tour, at the Roskilde Festival, Denmark. 'It's the most brutal experience we ever had,' recalls Eddie, still clearly shaken. 'I'm still trying to come to grips with it. Right before we went on that night, we got a phone call. Chris Cornell [vocalist of Soundgarden] and his wife, Susan, had a daughter that day. And also a sound guy left a day early, 'cause he was going to have a child. It brought me to tears, I was so happy. We were walking out on stage that night with two new names in our heads. And in 45 minutes everything changed.'

When the 50,000-strong crowd surged through a muddy field to try to gain better vantage points, the fans at the front of the stage took the brunt. 'The barrier was 30 metres away,' Stone recalls grimly, 'it was dark and raining. They'd been serving beer all day long. People fell down; the band had no idea.'

'There's been plenty of times in Pearl Jam's career where you see people go down and you stop the show,' confirmed Kelly. But this was not to be one of those times. Events very quickly turned to tragedy: as Pearl Jam played to the crowd, a number of fans were crushed and trampled underfoot in the melee. Eight of them were to die that night, while a ninth victim finally succumbed in hospital the following Wednesday.

It was redolent of the disaster that occurred when, on 3 December 1979, at the Riverfront Coliseum in Cincinnati, eleven Who fans had been trampled to death in a rush to the front before the band took the stage. 'I spoke yesterday to Eddie Vedder,' Townshend confirmed via his personal website. 'I passed on that I knew the Who had done wrong after the Cincinnati disaster – in a nutshell, I think we left too soon, and I spoke too angrily to the press and without proper consideration of the fact that the people who deserved respect were the dead and their families.

'Luckily Pearl Jam and their management have stayed in Denmark and cancelled subsequent shows. Other bands have also marked some respect by refusing to play.' Despite the band's conscientiousness, however, a report by local police to the Danish Ministry of Culture tried to hold them solely responsible for the tragedy. 'The reason those people died was that no one could get word out what was happening,' Kelly later protested. 'It was just chaos. There was a lot of Danish press that said we were inciting moshing. It wasn't during a crazy part of the set. It was during "Daughter".'

Based on interviews with 280 members of the audience, the police report concluded that the band had been 'whipping them up into a frenzy' by encouraging crowd surfing and other 'violent behaviour'. Despite clear evidence that the tragedy occurred when a contingent of the audience surged from a secondary stage to the main stage, where Pearl Jam were performing, the organisers were deemed blameless while the band's onstage demeanour was said to be at fault. 'We were part of an event that was disorganised on every level,' confirmed Stone. 'Mostly I feel like we witnessed a car wreck. But on another level, we were involved,' he conceded. 'You can't be there and not have some sense of being responsible. It's just impossible. All of us spent two days in the hotel in Denmark crying and trying to understand what was going on.'

'I find it hard to believe that after all that has transpired,' complained Kelly, 'the band's devastation over the tragedies that occurred at the Roskilde Festival during their performance, and their long history of attention to fan safety, that anyone would assign "moral responsibility" to them. That, I find appalling and ludicrous.'

Ultimately, no criminal charges against Pearl Jam would be filed by either the police or the ministry, but still the trauma took its toll. 'We saw a grief counsellor the next day and opened up about our feelings,' confirmed Mike, 'but it's torn a little part of all our lives. We'll never forget it. It was such an awful experience. You don't ever want to see anybody hurt at a show.'

'A couple of kids I saw at Roskilde, they're burned in my memory forever,' a haunted Jeff said later. 'Sometimes, when you're looking at a crowd, you can't help but see those faces.'

Of all the emotionally wounded band members, Eddie took the most earnestly direct route towards coming to terms with it: 'A friend of an Australian guy named Anthony Hurley asked if I would write something for the funeral. That was just hands-down the hardest thing I've ever had to do – not really knowing what was appropriate, not knowing how the family or friends felt; maybe I'm the last person they'd like to hear from. But it meant a lot to them, and it really helped me.'

As to whether the world tour should continue back in the US, it was briefly a moot point. 'Some of us thought maybe we should cancel the tour,' said Jeff. 'I felt if we cancel, what are we running from?' On Pearl Jam's return, however, a sign at a late August show in Camden, New Jersey, where they were supported by veteran noise-wavers/proto-grungers Sonic Youth, read: 'DUE TO THE NATURE OF MOSHING AND CROWD SURFING AND THE POSSIBLE INJURIES THAT COULD OCCUR, WE ASK THAT YOU REFRAIN FROM SUCH ACTIVITIES.'

'We're *not* going to play shows without seats,' insisted Mike. 'No standing shows. I just think if we did a standing show that I would look out there and it would be . . . too much,' he groped for the appropriate words.

Ultimately, Pearl Jam and the Danish police authorities resolved to meet in order to analyse what went wrong, on American soil. Scandinavian police representatives were invited to observe security arrangements at an early August gig in West Palm Beach, Florida, in the hope that the next Roskilde Festival could be made safer for the audience. As Pearl Jam's official press release on the event, issued two weeks earlier, had said: 'We owe it to everyone that has been impacted – all of those we lost, all of those who loved them, all of those who were injured and all of the fans who attend our performances – to identify every possible factor that might have contributed to these tragedies.

'It is our feeling that what happened at the Roskilde Festival cannot be written off entirely as a "freak accident" or "bad luck" as some have called it. When something this disastrous occurs, when this many lives are lost, it is essential that every aspect be examined thoroughly and from all angles.'

In addition to coping with the tragedy of lives needlessly lost at Roskilde, Eddie also had to endure the break up of his marriage to Beth Liebling. 'You can imagine what kind of foetal position I was in,' he recalled. 'I just remember thinking that there was no way out. I was listening to *The Who By Numbers* and there's a line in "Slip Kid" – "There's no easy way to be free." I was thinking, "I couldn't agree with you more."'

Pearl Jam's US leg of their 2000 world tour saw them re-affirm their commitment to social justice. In early November, their two shows at Seattle's Key Arena raised $500,000 to be divided among eighteen local and national charities.

As the early days of the new millennium moved into 2001, individual band members took a well-deserved hiatus and worked on their own personal side-projects. Mike McCready recorded an album with the Rockfords, described by him as 'a band of friends I've been playing with since I was eleven . . . It's a little pop, but with heavy tendencies – like some of the early eighties stuff I grew up on.' Matt Cameron recorded *The Scroll And Its Combinations* – his third album with the Wellwater Conspiracy, a part-time band also featuring guitarist John McBain, formerly of Monster Magnet, whose album featured a guest spot by former Soundgarden guitarist Kim Thayil. Stone Gossard became the first Pearl Jam member to release a solo album, with 2001's *Bayleaf* – an amalgam of classic rock and contemporary guitar sounds, quietly akin to Pearl Jam's recent work.

The comfortable cocoon of side-projects and inactivity into which the whole band had settled was abruptly rent asunder by the destruction of the World Trade Centre on 11 September 2001. Their reputation for social conscience and political activism ensured that the group quickly found that their reactions to the atrocity were keenly sought by the entertainment arm of the media – which was struggling to contextualise events far removed from its normal sphere. The intense outpouring of nationalism that followed in the collapsing towers' wake briefly served to drown out any possibility of dissent. For Eddie, this meant making a considered reaction once the shock-induced jingoism had subsided and it was again possible for opposition to US imperialism to be viewed as constructive, rather than anti-American. When asked by VH1 interviewer Gil Kaufman whether the band felt any necessity to comment creatively on the events of 9/11 Eddie replied, 'I've got a definitive answer and it's, "No." I certainly didn't feel a need to say, "Well, this is what *I* think, I gotta make sure to put down how it affected *me*."' However, despite telling Kaufman that he found many of the celebrity tributes to the disaster a turn-off, on 21 September, Eddie and Mike McCready joined Neil Young to perform 'Lost Road' at the network-spanning *A Tribute To Heroes* telethon. The show – which also included U2, Muhammad Ali, Will Smith, Tom Hanks and Stevie Wonder – was watched by an estimated 89 million viewers and raised around $30 million for the United Way's September 11 Telethon Fund. Mike and Eddie's performance was later included on the *A Tribute To Heroes* DVD, which was released on 4 December.

The following year, when the band recorded their seventh studio album at Seattle's Studio X, it proved difficult to prevent the impact of 9/11 seeping through. Despite avoiding any overt lyrical reference to the tragedy, Mike admitted to VH1 that 'it indirectly affected the recording sessions and all of us as musicians and people. I think we all changed that day. I wrote a song called "Last Soldier" that we played a bit around that time.'

On 22 October 2001 Pearl Jam substantiated rumours that they would re-emerge at the Groundwork 2001 benefit at the Seattle Key Arena. The concert, which also featured REM, Alanis Morissette and Qawwali vocal giant Rahat Nusrat Fateh Ali Khan, was the first North American event in the ongoing TeleFood campaign – an anti-hunger campaign initiated by the United Nations. With the weight of comeback expectation sobering his demeanour, Eddie strode into the spotlight dressed conservatively in a blue plaid suit and sober shirt, topped by a new, uncharacteristically short haircut. Any suggestion that the frontman's makeover was evidence of fading commitment to his beliefs was immediately dispelled as he launched into a searing cover of John Lennon's gritty 'Gimme Some Truth'. By the time the rest of Pearl Jam kicked in at the end of the first verse, the crowd were well on their way to an enthusiastic singalong. The momentum was maintained as the group thundered through 'Grievance' and 'Insignificance' with intensity and conviction. In addition to 'Insignificance', Pearl Jam showcased much of the *Binaural* material, as well as debuting an electric version of Eddie's hook-laden 'I Am Mine'. Having categorically demonstrated to the faithful that Pearl Jam were back – and firing on all cylinders – the band were joined by Rahat Nusrat Fateh Ali Khan for a celebratory, if shambolic, version of 'Long Road'.

After the gig, an upbeat Eddie explained that his new look made life significantly less complicated then the Mohawk he'd previously sported: 'With that last haircut I really asked for it. I was guaranteeing I was going to be searched on every plane I got on.'

Eddie's final public appearance of 2001 came the night after the Groundwork gig, when he joined REM – who were billed as the Minus 5 – for a surprise show at Seattle's Crocodile Café. In front of a small but enthusiastic gathering, Ed lent his unique vocals to versions of 'Long Road', 'Begin The Begin' and a medley of 'People Have The Power/It's The End Of The World As We Know It'. Stone Gossard saw out the year more energetically, taking Brad out on the road for a five-date tour that finished at the Seattle Showbox on 2 December.

The start of 2002 saw Pearl Jam baby-step their way toward recording *Riot Act*. After a two-week get together for 'pre-production' in February, the quintet once again went their separate ways. On 26 February Eddie turned in a solo set in support of the Concert for Artists' Rights benefit at the Wiltern Theatre in LA. Eddie and Mike McCready later joined Social Distortion mainman Mike Ness for a rendition of the Californian punks' 'Ball And Chain', before returning to the stage to accompany headliner Beck for an ensemble performance of the Stones' 'Sweet Virginia'. Despite hiding it under his hat for most of the show, it was evident that Eddie's Mohawk had been re-instated.

Three weeks later Ed made a speech inducting the Ramones into the Rock and Roll Hall of Fame, 'Yeah, I do have a Mohawk. No, I didn't get it to pose up here as a punk rocker for this exalted occasion,' he explained. 'It actually stems from my frustration with world events and bombings and things like that. I took it out on my own hair. Sometimes you feel powerless and you sometimes do silly things.' Since the Ramones had finally called it a day in 1996, Eddie had become close friends with 'da brudders' guitarist, Johnny Ramone. Despite the yawning ideological chasm between Ed's staunch liberalism and John's arch republicanism, the two surprisingly hit it off to the extent that Johnny presented Eddie with his guitar after the Ramones' final concert. During his speech, Eddie paid tribute to his friend. 'Johnny Ramone has been an extremely, extremely, great friend. His wife and he have been such a great friend to me, and taught me a lot about music that I was too young to see. Going back to the Brenda Lee comment and Gene Pitney, I was introduced to them by John. He has been a tutor of sorts.' When Johnny entered hospital with prostate cancer Ed was a regular visitor. Sadly, Johnny died on 15 September 2004. 'Never have I experienced a loss of someone I talked to with such frequency, in such depth, with such intimacy,' recalled Eddie.

When Pearl Jam reconvened on April Fools' Day to begin the serious work of lashing the new album together with REM, Soundgarden and Foo Fighters producer Adam Kasper, their mood was appropriately buoyant. Speaking to the *Seattle Times*'s Doug Pullen, Jeff Ament asserted that the break had been hugely beneficial. 'During our time away, everybody kind of has a little bit different life experience . . . when we do get back together and we haven't seen each other in a while, we're excited about that.' Jeff's feelings were echoed by Matt Cameron, who told *Seattle Post-Intelligencer* critic Gene Stout, 'The environment in the studio this time around was really good, really positive. Everyone came ready to work and we got a lot done in a fairly short amount of time.'

This upbeat atmosphere was abruptly shattered by the news that former Alice in Chains frontman Layne Staley had been found dead from a cocaine and heroin overdose. The revelation that Staley had lain undiscovered for a fortnight before being found only served to heighten the sense of waste and loss. Mike, who had formed Mad Season with Layne, spoke about Layne's long battle with addiction to Keith Ryan Cartwright of the *Tennessean*: 'I understand that mentality of, "Oh, I'm just going to keep doing it." It's a horrible disease, addiction or alcoholism, to get caught up in it and there's no way out. It's hard for me to judge Layne. I wish I had, I wish he had cleaned up. I was shocked to hear it. I mean a lot of people weren't, but I was saddened. Well, obviously saddened, but it was shocking.'

The night that news of Staley's death broke, Eddie recorded '4/20/02' – the title derived from the date of the fatal overdose – as a means of venting his frustration. 'That's Ed by himself,' recalled Mike in an interview with *Billboard*'s Jonathan Cohen, 'I got a call from Kelly [Curtis] that Layne died. We were in the studio at probably eleven at night. It was like, "Oh fuck." . . . Ed has this guitar kind of tuned like a banjo. He recorded it at like two or three in the morning, just with Adam. I think he was just so angry and he wanted to get it out.' The song would eventually emerge tucked away as a secret track on the *Lost Dogs* compilation the following year. 'I think the reason it's hidden is because he wouldn't want it to be exploitative,' observed Mike.

Despite this sudden shock, the quintet maintained brisk progress in the studio with Eddie continuing to channel his personal and political fury toward creative ends. 'I've never seen Ed work harder on lyrics,' enthused Mike. 'He'd run upstairs while we were in the studio and type out his lyrics and then come back down and cut them that night. And the next day he'd do the same thing. There wasn't ever a break for him.'

An additional element was added to the texture of *Riot Act* by keyboardist Kenneth 'Boom' Gaspar, who was to feature on close to half of the album's fifteen tracks. 'When there's keyboards you have to kind of play less on guitar,' Mike told MTV's Jon Wiederhorn. 'But having more keyboards was something I always wanted since having Brendan O'Brien play on "Betterman". It was a conscious effort to bring another sound into the equation.' Gaspar was introduced to the rest of the band by Eddie, who had met him on one of his frequent surfing trips to Hawaii. 'Boom made things pretty exciting. He's a super spiritual guy who kicks ass on keyboards,' bubbled Mike.

As well as the positive studio vibe, the *Riot Act* sessions were characterised by a more democratic approach to songwriting, initiated with *Yield*. Although Eddie continued to supply the lion's share of creativity – contributing to all bar three tracks – Jeff, Stone and Matt all weighed in with several songs. Far from feeling that he was losing his grip on the band's output, Eddie explained to *Seattle Weekly*'s Fred Mills that this approach was indicative of the band's increasing maturity. 'Now people come in with complete ideas, lyrics, complete songs, we just stick 'em all in the collective pot, and there's more than enough to go around and maintain a certain level. Trusting each other's tastes, I think, is good. And instincts, too. Instincts in how they approach a part. Because once you turn [a song] over to the group, you have to kind of let it go. It's learning how not to be abject at change.' This time around, Mike went against the flow by opting to reduce his lyrical input. 'I let Ed do that. I'm fully happy to have him sing lyrics over [the music] because he's really good at it,' he told the *Daily Nebraskan*'s Bart Schaneman.

Mike's sole writing co-credit on *Riot Act* was for the riff to 'Save You', which, as he revealed in an interview with *WMMR FM*'s Pierre Robert, came out of a jam with Stone. 'I had two ideas, and one idea I worked really hard on and thought it was totally great and then I played it for him, and he goes, "Well, that's . . . Okay. You got anything else?" And so, the other thing I had was the "Save You" riff, and he goes, "Oh, that's cool." . . . I was really built up to wanting to play this other song, and uh, nobody seemed to be very excited about it . . . but they were about the "Save You" riff.' The guitarist also penned 'Down', which failed to make the final *Riot Act* cut, but surfaced as the B-side of 'I Am Mine'. 'I wanted it to sound heavier than it actually did when we recorded it,' Mike explained. 'I liked how it came out, but it just didn't work with the rest of the record . . . Originally it was supposed to be more of a crunch-type thing. It just came out a little bit lighter than I thought. But people seem to dig it when we play it live. I'm proud of it. I like the song.'

More typical was Ed's continued emphasis on his lyrics reflecting events that deeply affected him – a basket of emotional influences that had now spread to include politics, mortality, relationships and feelings. 'It's everything from having a father who died when you were a kid to having nine people die in Roskilde to observing September 11,' he confided to *New York Daily News* journalist Isaac Guzman. 'Every year, we're losing a few people that we care about, people who have been adding something to the planet. It's part of what just seems meaningful when you sit down to write.' Mike enlarged upon the indirect nature of the creative impact of 9/11 on the album by explaining: 'The events that have happened since then were weighing heavily on our minds or had changed us emotionally and psychically. So there are some darker themes on this record and that's probably indicative of where some of those harder songs came from also.'

Ed's reactions to Roskilde were to find an outlet in three of the songs that made it onto *Riot Act*; 'I Am Mine', 'Love Boat Captain' and the primal angst of 'Arc'. 'Part of being comfortable as an artist is allowing yourself to experience those moments of transcendence, of some of the pain in the world,' Stone Gossard explained to Fred Mills. 'So you do have significant feelings of loss and pain and going through the death of friends and family. Those tend to be powerful images that come up when you're trying to write about things that are strong or powerful.'

Having backed Ralph Nader's doomed, liberal vote splitting presidential campaign in 2000, it was unsurprising that George W. Bush found himself squarely in the centre of Vedder's lyrical crosshairs. The result of this was 'Bushleaguer', which Ed co-wrote with Stone, a song that lampooned Bush's privileged upbringing – describing him as 'a confidence man' and attacking his post-9/11 policies through lyrics such as 'He's not a leader/ he's a Texas leaguer'. The lyrics are delivered in a spoken, sportscaster-style manner, complete with baseball metaphors, which serve to emphasise the satirical devices that Eddie employs to get his deadly serious points across. 'It was a personal view Ed had of the president, and it was very comical and a sort of theatre,' observed Stone in a *Milwaukee Journal Sentinel* interview.

Talking to *Rolling Stone*'s David Fricke the following year, Eddie revealed that the rest of the band were initially less than enthusiastic about the spoken-word elements of 'Bushleaguer'. 'The verses are real musical, really nice guitar, and I think they wanted it to be a song. They didn't want it to be ruined by some kind of spoken-word art piece . . . So I threw it on there, and they got to listen to it for a couple of weeks. I think they started to get used to it. They still put in a request: "Can you try it one more time? Can you say the same stuff, but sing it?" They finally came around.'

'Cropduster', a track for which Matt provided the music to Ed's lyrics, takes a more reflective, humanist view of the post-9/11 planet. Although the song contains lines such as 'This ain't no book you can close/ when the big lie hits your eye', Eddie's subtle use of pastoral metaphors proves that he can be just as effective when approaching his targets in a less confrontational manner. 'I think it's all about man's giant ego, that he's the most important thing on the planet. I don't know how it got so imbalanced,' Eddie told *The Onion AV* website's Josh Modell. 'At this point, we've got the power to destroy human life, and we're kind of cavalier about it, and it's gotten to the point where we've trivialised it into

"Showdown Against Iraq" or "Showdown In Iraq", as if it's the O.K. Corral and George W.'s got the below-the-waist belt buckled on, and he's gonna quick-draw somebody.'

In addition to criticising Bush's international expansionism, Eddie confronted Republican domestic policy on the grounds that the economics of the right were certain to widen the gulf between rich and poor. As well as being evident in 'Bushleaguer', this theme can be found within the environmental pleadings of 'Green Disease'. Similarly, the yawning chasm between the presentation and the reality of Bush's policies particularly irked Eddie. 'He prides himself on representing the people and being a guy you could have a beer with. But he absolutely represents corporate interests.'

By mid-summer, work on *Riot Act* was largely complete and the masters were duly handed over to Brendan O'Brien for mixing. Whilst Pearl Jam fansites speculated about the album's release date, the band returned to their side-projects – Ed made one of his occasional appearances as a guest of Neil Finn at the Seattle Showbox on 9 July, before appearing at a tribute gig for Who bass titan John Entwistle at Seattle's Chop Suey bar. Matt teamed up with Jodie Watts – a band formed from elements of the Rockfords – to play the Ramones' 'Blitzkrieg Bop' at the Seattle Central on 21 June, whilst Jeff backed jangle-rocker David Garza for his 20 June Showbox concert. Stone, who had been busy recording Brad's third album – *Welcome To Discovery Park* – took the band on a five-date mini-tour in mid-August. Mike had also been in the studio, where he joined Rob Zombie and a host of others to supply guitar for much of Zombie's Ramones tribute album, *We're A Happy Family*, for which Ed also contributed vocals to a cover of 'Daytime Dilemma'.

With *Riot Act* scheduled for a 12 November release, it came as no great surprise when Stone announced to the *Toronto Sun* that Pearl Jam were 'going to do a few shows sometime in late November and then probably in February'. On 22 August it was announced that 'I Am Mine' had been selected as the first single to be lifted from the new disc.

In early September the band took the surprising step of filming their first video since 'Given To Fly'. As part of a two-day rehearsal at the Chop Suey bar, director James Frost captured a performance of 'I Am Mine'. This represented a quantum shift in the quintet's promotional approach, which Mike explained to Gene Stout: 'We all sat down and said, "Hey, let's do some press. Let's try to promote this thing." But not to a sick level . . . In my mind, it's like when U2's last album came out. I thought if we could do like one-tenth of what those guys do and be as passionate about it, then hopefully people will get to hear the record.'

'I Am Mine' hit the airwaves three weeks ahead of its 8 October release date, and quickly became a radio hit. Once in the stores, the single sold reasonably well, but failed to trouble the upper reaches of the *Billboard* chart, peaking at Number 26. This was of little concern to Mike McCready, who was just grateful to still be around, 'I'm amazed that people are even still wanting to listen to us. With all the other music out there and the shifting times, I'm surprised that people still consider us relevant. I'll hear us on classic rock radio stations and I'll go, "Oh, my God, we're getting old!"'

As plans for a mammoth five-month 2003 world tour coalesced, Ed, Jeff, Mike and Matt blew off some of the live cobwebs by supporting the Who with a ten-song set at the House of Blues, Chicago, on 23 September. Two days later Ed teamed up with Bruce Springsteen to duet on 'My Hometown' at the veteran rocker's Chicago show.

Chartwise, *Riot Act* did a little better than its preceding single, debuting at Number 5 on the US chart, before beginning a gentle slide that saw the album drop out of the Top Forty in mid-December. Two days after the disc's release, Pearl Jam again gingerly dipped their collective toes in promotional waters with a pair of appearances on *The Late Show With David Letterman*. The quintet delivered a polished, if reserved, rendition of 'I Am Mine', before returning to give 'Save You' an airing the following night.

Although the band were keen to reach people, chart success was a distant priority behind creating an atmosphere within the group that was conducive to making good music. 'They all kind of have lives and they're a little older now and they've gotten to this real comfortable way of being in a band,' observed Kelly Curtis. 'It's something that's really healthy. Everybody's okay with it.'

Riot Act was accorded a mixed reception by the music press, whereas *Billboard*'s Jonathan Cohen enthused that the album 'bulges with a host of showcases for Pearl Jam's signature rock power', *Rolling Stone*'s Keith Harris described the sound as 'tired', observing that Eddie 'cautiously mutters his vocals as though a baby is asleep in the next room'. Such criticisms hardly registered within the band, despite their having held out an olive branch of accessibility to the usually hostile media. 'We've learned how to balance everything out now in terms of how much you live in the press world and how much time you live making music with your friends,' observed Stone. 'And a bit more about what your personal priorities are. That helps a lot.'

As a warm-up for the world tour, which was scheduled to kick off in Brisbane on 8 February, a quartet of Seattle shows were arranged. Two gigs at the Showbox on 5-6 December were followed by a pair of benefits at the Key Arena in support of a broad range of local causes including the Vera Project, Home Alive, Lifelong AIDS Alliance and the Seattle Centre Arts Academy. Support was provided by Brad on both nights, with fellow grunge survivors Mudhoney replacing Steve Earle for the second gig. Although the broiling mosh-pits of the mid-nineties had been replaced by more static forms of appreciation, Fred Mills noted that 'the Pearl Jam concert experience is still loaded with passion and energy'.

The release of *Riot Act* marked the end of Pearl Jam's deal with Epic, and although the label were planning an album of rarities and B-sides, neither band nor record company seemed in any hurry to extend their relationship. As Kelly Curtis attested, 'I don't think we're feeling any desperate need to have a deal. If anything, it's the opposite. We're kind of looking forward to not owing ourselves to anybody or anything.' It wasn't as if the faithful were likely to be deprived of product – as on previous outings, the band had decided to release their own 'bootleg' versions for each of the upcoming gigs. To keep the pot boiling singles-wise, 'Save You', backed with 'Other Side', was released on 11 February, without making any dent on the upper reaches of the US chart.

If proof of Pearl Jam's continuing global popularity was needed, the huge roar with which their arrival was greeted by the 12,500-strong crowd at the Brisbane Entertainment Centre was more than sufficient. The 8 February show marked the start of ten dates, which constituted the Australian leg of the tour. Support was provided by ex-Smith Johnny Marr, and his band the Healers. Although some first-night nerves were in evidence, with Ed forgetting the odd line and joking with the crowd about the gig being 'our rehearsal', the two-hour set was enthusiastically received. The band showcased around half of the songs from *Riot Act* as well as dipping into their back catalogue for old favourites such as 'Even Flow'.

Aside from some minor grumbles about the thuggish antics of security staff at Melbourne, the energising pattern established by the opening gig was continued as Pearl Jam worked through their itinerary of Australia's major cities. After a final show at the Burswood Dome in remote Perth, where Johnny Marr joined the group for an encore of Creedence Clearwater Revival's 'Fortunate Son', band and crew rushed to catch their flights to Japan, where a show at Sun Plaza was set for the following night.

As in Australia, the *Riot Act* material went down well with Japanese audiences who were delighted to have the opportunity to see the band at last. However, once the tour returned to the US, the anti-Bush sentiments of 'Bushleaguer' got under the skin of a few rednecks. At the 1 April concert at Denver's Pepsi Centre, a section of the crowd booed and even walked out when Eddie recounted a conversation with a Vietnam veteran who doubted the legitimacy of the US invasion of Iraq and impaled a mask of George W. on his mic-stand during a performance of 'Bushleaguer'. Although an official statement declared: 'It's possible two dozen left during the encore, but it was not noticeable amongst the 11,976 who were loudly applauding and enjoying the evening's music. It just made a better headline to report otherwise.' Jeff subsequently told Mike Keefe-Feldman of the *Missoula Independent* that 'about twenty or thirty percent of the people were booing loudly. So it was definitely something that none of us had experienced before.' The furore put Mike in something of a difficult position, as his cousin was part of Bush's invading task force. 'I know Mike was pretty upset about it and said some things about not wanting to play ['Bushleaguer'] again. I think the booing kind of got to him a little bit harder. And maybe he isn't totally in line with the way that Ed thinks and the way I think, and that's all part of being in a band or a relationship: communicating your differences.'

On the night, Eddie asserted his First Amendment rights – to cheers and applause from the majority of the crowd. 'I don't know if you heard about this thing – it's called freedom of speech, man. It's worth thinking about it because it's going away. In the last year of being able to use it, we're sure as fuck going to use it and I'm not going to apologise.' During the encore, Ed made a placatory attempt to explain his position. 'Just to clarify . . . we support the troops. We're just confused about how wanting to bring them back safely all of a sudden becomes non-support . . . They're not the ones who make the foreign policy. They're just doing their jobs.'

The inevitable shit-storm of knee-jerk caterwauling followed from flag-waving sections of the press, with Scripps Howard News reporter Mark Bowen opining that Vedder's criticism of US foreign policy went 'too far', insisting that the singer had also swung the mask of Bush in the air and 'stomped on it'. Pearl Jam and their management countered that such reports were 'overblown'. 'The beauty of that first show is the crowd was totally into it,' recounted Jeff in an interview with Newhouse News Service journalist Doug Pullen. 'The crazy thing is because of what the media generated there, it turned into this negative thing.' Later Mike, who confessed to the *Detroit Free Press*'s Ben Edmonds that he was '*so* tired of talking about this', demonstrated his solidarity by declaring, 'This band has arguments all the time – about politics, music, everything. Ask us a question and you're likely to get five different answers. But Ed is our focal point, and we support him completely.'

While events at Denver served to ram home the complexities of dissent in a post-9/11 environment, the fact that 'Bushleaguer' had caused no reaction whatsoever in Australia and Japan served to highlight the increasing global isolation that the Bush Administration's policies were inflicting on America. Jeff added further context by observing, 'The headline said "Dozens jam the exits". In our mind, it made it seem like a small riot with fans jamming the exits. Who would be more sensitive to that? We just got through with Roskilde.'

Within a fortnight, the furore had died down as the *Riot Act* tour made its way across the southern US. Bush's supporters had a whole planet of opposition to rail against and the Seattle frontman was just one of literally millions of voices joined in opposition against their president's transparent and wasteful military exercise.

As April wore on, Pearl Jam entered America's industrial heartland. With well over 30 dates still remaining before the trek's end, and only a brief break between dates in Pennsylvania and Missoula in early- to mid-May, Ed worked hard at rotating the band's catalogue as a means of keeping things fresh. 'You can see him start to scribble sometime in afternoon, whether it's when we're flying in or on the way to the soundcheck,' revealed Stone in an interview with *Pittsburgh Tribune-Review*'s Regis Behe. 'Sometimes it's ten minutes before we're going on. It's based on, one, what's our mood tonight, and two, on what didn't we play the night before.'

Pearl Jam finally wrapped up their lengthy North American tour arc with a gig at the PNC Arts Centre in Holmdale, New Jersey on 14 July 2003. The final three concerts of the entire tour were to take place in Mexico, where the band held a rare press conference, during which Mike enthused about playing the country for the first time. When the tour was over, the quintet once again returned to their individual musical pursuits, secure in the knowledge that they had now attained the position of a band whose following had matured along with them and relieved that the hysteria of mass success had dissipated, allowing them to follow their own paths, free from label influence or excessive fan pressure.

In October, Pearl Jam reunited for an acoustic benefit in aid of the YouthCare charity, which sold out in eight minutes flat, despite little promotion. The performance was subsequently issued as an album in July 2004. Titled *Live At Benaroya Hall October 22nd 2003*, the disc was distributed via BMG and the Ten Club with a proportion of sales being donated to YouthCare.

Three further shows followed in California, all in aid of similarly good causes. The following month, Epic released *Lost Dogs*, a sprawling 31-track compilation of rarities, B-sides and tracks from benefit albums. As far as Mike was concerned, this material represented the tip of an unreleased iceberg. 'We have vaults and vaults of this stuff,' he observed. A *Pearl Jam Live At The Garden* DVD was issued on the same day (11 November), featuring the band's 8 July show at Madison Square Garden.

Before the group could settle into their planned break, they contributed a new song, 'Man Of The Hour', to the soundtrack of Tim Burton's movie *Big Fish*. The track was released as a single which, although not a massive hit, enjoyed healthy global sales and was subsequently nominated for a Golden Globe in the 'Best Original Song' category.

On 11 June 2004, whilst the group were on extended hiatus, Eddie became a father for the first time. His new partner, model Jill McCormick, gave birth to a baby girl, Olivia. Naturally, the vocalist was delighted at the new arrival, prompting Stone to observe, 'Ed's in a better space than I've ever seen him.'

Pearl Jam returned to live action with a run of a dozen US gigs during September and October. The shows were part of the Vote For Change tour, a series of concerts in marginal states designed to swing the forthcoming electoral vote against George W. Bush. Although the tour attracted healthy audiences to catch performances by such diverse acts as blues guitarist Keb' Mo', REM, the Dixie Chicks, Bruce Springsteen and the E Street Band, and James Taylor, the event had little impact at the polls.

In addition to their political content, the Vote For Change concerts were notable for the inclusion of a solo performance from

Eddie ahead of the main event. This practice was instigated at the 24 September Showbox gig in Seattle, where Eddie opened with a rendition of Cat Stevens' reflective ballad 'Don't Be Shy'. Eddie's choice of song was motivated by his disgust for the way in which the US authorities had recently denied Stevens – who had converted to the Islamic faith and adopted the name Yusuf in 1977 – entry into America on the basis that his name appeared on a 'No-Fly' list of supposed Muslim extremists. At subsequent shows Eddie performed a varied selection of songs including the Beatles' 'You've Got To Hide Your Love Away', Steven Van Zandt's 'I Am A Patriot' and Springsteen's 'Growin' Up'.

Pearl Jam also assimilated a slew of incendiary cover versions into their own set, with numbers such as US proto-punks the Germs' 'Lion's Share', John Lennon's 'Gimme Some Truth', and the classic MC5 number 'Kick Out The Jams' getting an airing alongside the surprise inclusion of old favourites such as 'Alone', which hadn't featured on the set list for almost a decade. When the quintet made a short-notice appearance on the 30 September edition of *The Late Show With David Letterman*, the covers motif was extended with a performance of Bob Dylan's pacifist anthem 'Masters Of War'.

After the Vote For Change tour wrapped up in mid-October, Pearl Jam again went their separate ways. Eddie showed up onstage at a Springsteen concert on 13 October and along with Mike made a guest appearance at the Seattle leg of Michael Moore's Slacker Uprising tour six days later.

Two thousand and five began with Eddie appearing alongside Queens of the Stone Age and Eagles of Death Metal mainstay Josh Homme, Dave Grohl and Beck at a 17 January tsunami relief concert in Los Angeles, designed to raise funds for Red Cross efforts to provide relief for those whose lives had been devastated by the Indian Ocean earthquake less than a month earlier.

The band remained without a label, and although plans to record an eighth studio album were being tentatively outlined, there was as yet little sign of a recording contract on the horizon. To keep the creative pot boiling, the quintet hooked up for a small show at Seattle's Paramount Theatre that marked the 25th anniversary of Stone's alma mater, the Northwest School, where they debuted a new number, 'Crapshoot Rapture', which latterly re-emerged as 'Comatose' in 2006.

In late April, Pearl Jam played a sixteen-song set in support of the Coalition of Independent Music Stores at Easy Street Records in Seattle. Seven of the numbers performed that night were selected for inclusion on a mini-album, *Live At Easy Street*, which was released exclusively to independent retailers the following year. Again, cover versions comprised a significant proportion of the set, with high-octane punk classics such as the Avengers' 'American In Me' and the Dead Kennedys' 'Bleed For Me', making it onto the disc.

The same month, the group announced that they would be reuniting later in the year for a fifteen-date Canadian tour, kicking off in Vancouver on 2 September and wrapping up in St John's, Newfoundland, three weeks later. Demand for tickets proved to be reassuringly high and within a month the group were compelled to add extra dates. With no label to release 'official bootlegs' it was decided that downloads of the shows would be made available from their official website within hours of the concerts ending.

At the end of August, with four US dates now tacked onto the end of their Canadian trek, Pearl Jam blew away their live cobwebs with a pair of warm-up shows. The first, at Missoula, Montana, was a benefit in support of Democratic senate candidate Jon Tester's ultimately successful campaign. Although, by American standards, Tester represented something of a liberal, being critical of George Bush's occupation of Iraq, the buzz-cut junior senator's opposition to same-sex marriages and disapproval of abortion made him a slightly curious beneficiary of the band's support.

The second concert, on 1 September, represented something of a homecoming for the band, as it was the first time that they had performed at the Gorge in Washington for twelve years. Pleased to be back, the quintet weighed in with a mighty three-hour, half-acoustic, half-electric set that encompassed some 36 songs.

The Canadian tour was a concrete demonstration of the way in which Pearl Jam had developed into a touring band with few peers; the gigs were celebratory events drawing upon the band's significant back catalogue and broad corpus of influences. As well as support from Washington indie rockers Sleater-Kinney, the tour also extended Eddie's practice of appearing ahead of the main event to perform solo.

After five shows in Pittsburgh, Atlantic City, Philadelphia and the House of Blues in Chicago at the beginning of October (where support was provided by Led Zep legend Robert Plant), the band took six weeks out to work on new material and prepare for a thirteen-date tour of Chile, Argentina, Brazil and Mexico that had been announced at the start of September.

Supported by grunge trailblazers Mudhoney, the South/Latin American tour began at the 20,000-capacity Estadio San Carlos de Apoquindo in Santiago, Chile on 22 November. Usually the home to soccer team Deportivo Universidad CatóÛlica, the packed stadium provided the band with the kind of welcome more generally associated with victorious sports heroes, with supportive chants from the crowd and singalongs spontaneously breaking out throughout the set. During the show – which featured a cover of 'Blitzkrieg Bop' – Eddie paid tribute to the departed members of the Ramones, while the crowd responded with chants of 'Ramones! *Hola* Johnny! *Hola* Joey! *Hola* Dee Dee!'

The celebratory atmosphere continued throughout the tour, with Matt Cameron's 43rd birthday being celebrated on stage at the Gigantinho Gymnasium, Porto Alegre, Brazil, with an impromptu birthday-cake fight and Eddie addressing the Rio crowd a week later with a halting Portuguese declaration that, 'Next time we play in Brazil the world will be a better place 'cause George Bush won't be president anymore.'

Although attendances at some of the Mexican shows were a little disappointing – with Monterrey's cavernous Auditorio Coca Cola being less than half full, the tour was a palpable success, demonstrating the band's enduring popularity far beyond their home turf.

After the final Mexican date on 10 December, Pearl Jam returned to the US for the holiday season. As usual the band released a special festive offering for Ten Club members – this year it was a single featuring a cover version of Elvis Presley's 1961 cut 'Little Sister' that had been recorded at the Chicago House of Blues in October and included Robert Plant on backing vocals. The track was backed with the as-yet-unreleased 'Gone'.

In February 2006, 74-year-old former Columbia Records president and Arista Records founder Clive Davis announced that he had signed Pearl Jam to his J Records label. Ironically, like Epic, J Records is part of the massive Sony BMG conglomerate. However, although the group had held talks with smaller, apparently more credible labels such as Epitaph, Eddie maintained that the decision to sign with J was a simple matter of practicalities. 'It just came down to something like distribution. Everything else we do in-house, anyway,' he told *Magnet* magazine's Eric T. Miller. 'It's just a matter of how to get the songs into people's hands so they can get it into their ears. That – and not being represented in a way that we find offensive – is what it comes down to for us.'

Within a month of Davis's announcement, the first new Pearl Jam studio offering in over three years manifested in the shape of the 'World Wide Suicide' single. Released on 14 March as a digital download, the track was backed with another new song, 'Unemployable', that would also feature on the band's forthcoming J Records debut.

'World Wide Suicide' had been released to radio stations just over a week ahead of its official issue and created an immediate impact, picking up just under 2,000 plays on modern rock stations in a mere seven days. The track was also made available as a free download via the Pearl Jam website and entered the *Billboard* Modern Rock Chart at Number 3 in mid-March, climbing to the top spot the following week.

The band's first Number 1 single of any kind since 1996's 'Who You Are', the release of 'World Wide Suicide' was accompanied by a video that interspersed performance footage with scenes of Chilean street performer Sebastián González shot backstage at the Estadio San Carlos de Apoquindo the previous November.

Directed by photographer and filmmaker Danny Clinch, who had previously collaborated with Dave Grohl's Foo Fighters and photographed the likes of Johnny Cash, Bruce Springsteen and Tupac Shakur, the promo – along with performances of the track on *Letterman* and *Saturday Night Live* – was indicative of the band's newfound rationale of using the media as a means of getting their anti-war, anti-Bush messages heard. 'It seems like a critical time to participate in our democracy,' Eddie told *Rolling Stone*'s Brian Hiatt. 'I think we're representatives of America. We certainly have as much clout as, well, Rush Limbaugh. So if he's gonna fuckin' blow hot air, using his platform, then we should be doing the same.'

By the time Pearl Jam had finalised their deal with J Records, the new album had been recorded and mastered during a series of sessions at Studio X that had taken place throughout the winter months. With only the album art and packaging left to be finalised, the label announced a 2 May release for what was to be a thirteen-track, self-titled disc.

Again produced by Adam Kasper, *Pearl Jam* immediately signals its hard-rocking intentions with the powerful, solo-laden 'Life Wasted'. Lyrically, the song can be interpreted as Eddie mining his feelings of loss over the death of Johnny Ramone. 'I think that song is there to remind you, "This is that feeling,"' explained Vedder. 'The truth is – I'm a little sensitive and this is a close, personal relationship. I'll just say it. Fuck it. Right up front. Half the record is based on the loss of the guy who turned out to be the best friend I ever had on the planet. And that was Johnny Ramone.'

'Life Wasted' was selected as the second single to be culled from the album and promoted via a sumptuous video directed by Fernando Apodaca, who also designed *Pearl Jam*'s liner art. Fittingly, the video was nominated for an MTV Music Video Award for special effects later in the year.

Better known as an artist than a filmmaker, Apodaca created a series of rich, nightmarish images of the band in various states of decomposition, using sculpture and mapping to create an almost elemental depiction of decay and entropy. 'He's all-around, refuses to be pigeonholed, works with every medium there is,' Eddie told *Rolling Stone*'s Austin Scaggs. 'Line drawings with hair to stitching up leather bodices . . . everything is very organic. I think the only reason he hasn't made a name for himself in the art world is that he holds the art world in contention. I've talked to him, and I think the fact he has a high respect for us is a high compliment.'

After the apocalyptic 'World Wide Suicide' comes 'Comatose', which had been performed live as 'Crapshoot Rapture' over a year earlier. Raw and fast paced, the track is a 140-second burst of anger, angst and defiance that matches Mike's discordant soloing with Eddie's vocal gymnastics.

Described by Vedder as being 'about psychotropics', 'Severed Hand' begins with some suitably psychedelic-sounding, reverse-recorded guitar before emerging as a driving, wah-wah infused exploration of hedonism and humanity. Amazingly, the lyrics had been composed by Eddie almost six years earlier. 'I started writing that one in a hotel room in Virginia the same night I wrote "I Am Mine",' he revealed in an interview with *Billboard*'s Jonathan Cohen. 'I had it around for years and didn't know where it was supposed to go next. I think we even tried doing a bit of it for *Riot Act* but probably didn't spend more than an hour or two on it. It had been sitting in port for a while.'

In addition to lyrics that hint at Ed's disapproval of America's imperialist foreign policy, 'Marker In The Sand' is notable for Mike's unusually resonant guitar sound. '"Marker" came from a really odd tuning. It's this bizarre tuning that I kind of got from Mark Arm of Mudhoney when we were on tour with them, and I just kind of started messing around with it,' he explained to *Seattle Post-Intelligencer* critic Gene Stout. 'It forced me to play a different way.'

The thunderous impact of *Pearl Jam*'s opening clutch of songs is disrupted by the relaxed acoustic 'Parachutes', a gentle recountment of loss and regret that comes as something of a surprise after the *sturm und drang* that precedes it. The track is followed by the blue-collar soap opera of 'World Wide Suicide' B-side 'Unemployable.' A mid-tempo slice of Springsteen-esque social comment, the song picks up the energy levels ahead of the fierce power of 'Big Wave'.

Drawing some influence from Pete Townshend's 1972 solo cut 'Let's See Action', 'Gone' explores the anti-materialistic element of leaving one's past behind and moving on. 'The idea was that this guy was leaving Atlantic City and needing to find a new life without his past, without his possessions, and not really looking for more possessions,' Eddie explained. 'Because it takes place in a car, it's probably very similar to "Rearviewmirror" in a way.'

After the brief 'Wasted Reprise' comes 'Army Reserve', an evocative description of those who wait at home while fathers, brothers and sons go to war. The song features lyrics co-written by Damien Wayne Echols, who achieved notoriety when he was sentenced to death by lethal injection for his alleged involvement in the murders of three eight-year-old boys in West Memphis, Arkansas during 1993.

Accused along with two others, Jessie Misskelley and Jason Baldwin, Echols never stopped protesting his innocence, insisting that a miscarriage of justice had taken place. All three men, he maintained, had been tried amid an unfair atmosphere of media scrutiny and moral panic. Subsequently the trio – dubbed 'The West Memphis Three' by the media – became something of a *cause célèbre*, with the likes of Winona Ryder, Henry Rollins, Joe Strummer and Tom Waits throwing their weight behind efforts to clear them of their supposed crimes. In July 2007, new forensic evidence would be presented to exonerate Echols, Misskelley and Baldwin at long last.

Pearl Jam's penultimate track, 'Come Back', is a simple love song that drifts by pleasantly ahead of the epic, valedictory 'Inside Job' – notable for being the first time that Mike's lyrics had graced a Pearl Jam album. Described by *Rolling Stone* heavyweight David Fricke as being 'like a combination of "Stairway To Heaven" and the Who's "The Song Is Over"', McCready's lyrics indicate a man seeking to resolve his inner conflicts. 'I'd been thinking about some stuff for a year or two and searching for kind of a spiritual answer to whatever maladies were in my life,' revealed Mike. 'I realised that I had to go inside myself first before I could be open to outside ideas. And that's kind of what the premise was.'

The album was released to something approaching universal acclaim, with many commentators identifying the disc as Pearl Jam's strongest work since *Vitalogy*, or even *Vs.* In his *Rolling Stone* review, David Fricke observed that the LP was the band's best for a decade. 'We've heard a lot of that,' declared Eddie. 'And, you know, if that needs to be said in order to prick up someone's ears and say, "I'll have to revisit this band," then I don't think we can complain about it.'

Mike attributed the energised nature of *Pearl Jam* to the band's fresh start with a new label. 'When we wrote these songs we were feeling fresh and energetic and we were communicating better than ever. So the music just kind of happened. It harkens back to the energy of our second record, I believe. But I think J Records is also doing a really good job of promoting the record and getting it played on the radio and getting fans excited about it. Everything's kind of firing on all cylinders.'

For his part, Clive Davis was more than upbeat about the band's apparent renaissance. 'They're fresh, they're hungry and they're loaded for bear,' he insisted.

Commercially, Davis's confidence in his new charges proved well founded – *Pearl Jam* stormed up the *Billboard* chart, racking up an impressive 279,000 copies sold in the first week following its release. The disc peaked at Number 2 and reached the Top Ten in Canada, Britain, New Zealand, Ireland, Australia and Germany.

Buoyed by waves of critical and popular approval, the quintet headed out on their biggest tour for several years. After a warm-up date at New York's Irving Plaza on 5 May, the band headed north to Toronto for a pair of shows, before playing a further fifteen gigs during the first leg of their US Tour. The roadshow then took a three-week break ahead of a run of 22 shows in a month, which climaxed with two homecoming concerts at the Gorge Amphitheatre in Washington. 'I think it's one of my top three favourite places to play in the world,' enthused Mike. 'The drive's a little bit of a pain in the butt, but you get to see the Columbia River Gorge behind you as you're standing on stage and then you look up and see all these screaming fans looking the other way. There's nothing quite like it. It's quite spiritual and it's quite fun and rocking.'

Following a gig at Dublin's massive Point venue on 23 August, Pearl Jam made their first festival appearances since the Roskilde tragedy when they headlined the Reading and Leeds events on the 25 and 27 August. Understandably, Eddie opened both shows by appealing to the crowd to remain calm and 'look after each other'. To the band's evident relief, both shows passed off without any untoward incidents.

After late August appearances in Belgium and Holland, September saw the group tour continental Europe for the first time since 2000, visiting eight countries before finishing the jaunt at the OAKA Sports Hall, Athens on the final day of the month.

In November, the tour took on truly global dimensions, as Pearl Jam travelled to Australia for a dozen shows supported by indie-billies the Kings of Leon. The Australian dates included a surprise appearance at a Make Poverty History event in Melbourne, where the band were joined onstage by Bono and The Edge from U2. Finally, the road marathon was rounded out with a trio of dates in Hawaii, finishing in Honolulu on 9 December.

The majority of the shows on the tour were sold out and without exception the concerts were warm, celebratory events, with the individual members of Pearl Jam demonstrating a hard-won stability alongside their evident musical and personal maturity. 'The fact that we're still around is icing on the cake,' reflected Mike. 'It's been more than fifteen years and we have a new record and people seem to be excited about it. I've always had the belief that the band could be over tomorrow. It's just the nature of how bands are. And somehow we've been able to make it last. There's a feeling that, wow, we're really lucky.'

This sense of collective stability enabled individual band members to pursue solo projects with renewed assurance. During the summer, Eddie had contributed a number of acoustic songs to Sean Penn's adaptation of Jon Krakauer's book *Into The Wild*, which hit American screens in September 2007.

The movie featured *Lords Of Dogtown* star Emile Hirsch as Christopher McCandless, a traveller who cut his ties with family and friends to explore the Alaskan wilderness, where he ultimately died of starvation in 1992. Initially, Eddie had considered taking a role in the film. '[Penn] asked me and I said yeah, because he can be very convincing,' he told *Billboard*'s Jonathan Cohen. 'Then I came to my senses. For one thing, it was a great opportunity and I would probably do it just to spend time with Sean. But if you get past that, I always felt like a lot of people watching would be thinking, "Wow, this guy took the job of a working actor. [*laughs*] Why does he need another job?"'

After viewing a rough cut of the film, Vedder set to work at Studio X with Adam Kasper. 'I'd just sit in the chair, and they'd hand me a fretless bass, and they'd hand me a mandolin, and they'd take a second to do the rough mix, and then I'd write the vocal, and it was just quick,' explained Eddie in an interview with *Time*'s Lev Grossman. 'It was like I kinda went into some weird space for a week or two, and then I woke up out of this daze, and it was done.'

Eddie's soundtrack was released through J Records as an eleven-track CD, which hit the *Billboard* chart at Number 11 in late September. The critical reception for the disc slanted marginally toward the positive, with *Rolling Stone*'s David Fricke observing: 'Eddie Vedder tells the young man's story on the soundtrack to Sean Penn's *Into The Wild*, tossing his weighty baritone onto earthy, folky tracks that temper the romance of absolute freedom with an eerie foreboding. Vedder strikes a cinematic tone on the jangly opener, "Setting Forth", and ten more sketches that evoke days spent contemplating a vast skyline.'

Eddie subsequently shot a video for the disc's final track 'Guaranteed', which was directed by Mark Rocco – best known for writing and directing the 2005 post-Iraq War psychodrama *The Jacket*. 'I hope that I've portrayed visually the song "Guaranteed" in a way that leaves the viewer as emotionally moved as I was the first time I heard Eddie's music for *Into The Wild*,' enthused Rocco. Such was the affecting nature of 'Guaranteed' that it scooped a Golden Globe for Best Song Written For A Motion Picture.

In December, it was announced that Eddie would be contributing music to a documentary entitled *The People Speak*, adapted from Howard Zinn's *A People's History Of The United States*. The vocalist also made an appearance in the documentary, alongside the likes of Sean Penn, Matt Damon, Bob Dylan and Morgan Freeman. Filming began in Boston during January and the feature would eventually be released in December 2009.

While Eddie was otherwise engaged, the rest of Pearl Jam occupied themselves by recording a re-working of Bill Haley and the Comets' 1954 standard 'Rock Around The Clock', which was subsequently aired on the band's official website. Entitled 'Rock Around Barack', the song represented a demonstration of support for the Democratic presidential candidate Barack Obama. When Obama was swept into the White House on waves of hysterical public support in November, Vedder declared himself 'so overwhelmed and overcome with emotion . . . I feel incredible, I feel relieved, I feel exhausted.'

As America congratulated itself on electing a president not obviously bent on world domination, Eddie seized the mood of optimism with gusto. 'Two years ago, you were wondering what could there possibly be to unite our country and get us out of this mess. What can get us back on the positive? What can bring us back into some kind of standing with the international community? And it seemed like there would not be any answer. Who knew we would get to this moment?' he gushed in an interview with *Metronews.ca* journalist Alan Cross. 'Now it's up to us to keep that candle, turn that into a flame and keep it burning. And to protect and serve him and serve our nation now that the electorate has been invigorated.'

In April 2008, as Obama's presidential campaign gathered its unstoppable populist momentum, Eddie took his solo material out on the road for a seven-date tour that saw him travelling south from Vancouver to San Diego supported by New Zealand-born singer-songwriter Liam Finn. 'I've known Eddie since I was about ten or eleven years old,' explained Finn, who is the eldest son of Crowded House frontman Neil Finn. 'He's kind of a friend of the family, I suppose.'

Eddie had prepared for the tour by performing an unscheduled set for Seattle-based fans who'd bought tickets for an advance screening of *Into The Wild*. Mixing solo material with Pearl Jam favourites, Vedder also strapped on a banjo to perform a version of Cat Stevens' 'If You Want To Sing Out, Sing Out'. 'He's going to do great,' observed Jeff Ament. 'He's been warming up for this his whole life, but especially the last seven or eight years, playing a song or two himself before our shows.' While Eddie was hitting the road, both Jeff and Stone Gossard were working on solo albums that would see release later in the year.

Further Vedder solo material surfaced on *Body Of War: Songs That Inspired An Iraq War Veteran*. Released on Sire, the two-disc compilation was conceived as a companion to the documentary of the same name that focused on Tomas Young, an American soldier who was paralysed from the waist down by a bullet wound sustained during the Iraq conflict. In addition to Eddie and Ben Harper's live version of 'No More', recorded during the Chicago leg of the 2007 Lollapalooza Tour, a concert recording of Pearl Jam's version of Black Sabbath's classic 'Masters Of War' also made the collection, alongside contributions from such diverse acts as Tori Amos, Public Enemy, Neil Young and System of a Down. Profits from the album benefited Iraq Veterans Against the War, a cause personally selected by Young. 'Tomas has taught me a great deal,' declared Eddie. 'It has been a mind-expanding experience. I see how he relies on the strength of the songs to help him through each day. It is a true living example of the power of music.'

After Eddie's solo tour had successfully concluded in San Diego, Pearl Jam reconvened ahead of a ten-date summer tour set to begin on 11 June in West Palm Beach, Florida. The group got together to rehearse and try out new ideas for their next album. 'It doesn't mean there'll be a record out next month, but it's the start of the process,' explained Jeff. 'Sometimes it takes six months and sometimes it takes two years. It's just fun to play – we've actually gotten really good at jamming with each other, so it's fun to get together and crank up the amps. We'll have Matt throw a beat at us and try to come up with something. There's some new, different kind of things coming out of people.'

The band were joined by producer Brendan O'Brien and worked on 'four or five' new songs. 'He's a super pro,' enthused Jeff. 'I've always felt, working with him, that he understood me as a bass player and that's not always easy. A lot of producers are there to please the singer. But I've always had a great rapport with him. I can tell him I want something to sound like the O'Jays or Led Zeppelin or PJ Harvey and he gets it.'

As the June tour got underway, Pearl Jam struck a deal with Verizon Wireless's V Cast service to sell select tracks from authorised 'live bootlegs' of the shows. The tracks were made available as dual downloads that would be sent to both the mobile phones and computers of anyone purchasing them.

The stand-out gig of the tour was the band's headlining spot at the Bonnaroo Festival, in Manchester, Tennessee, which saw Eddie follow an impassioned rendering of Dylan's 'All Along The Watchtower', with an equally heartfelt speech promoting the 'Vote For Change' ideal. 'It is welded into the constitution that people have not only the right, but the responsibility to make change,' he declared. 'It can't get any worse. We're right here in the middle of America. We can change the whole world.' The show was also notable for being only the second time that Pearl Jam had made a large-scale festival appearance since Roskilde. 'There was a time when we thought we'd never play a show like this again – and for good reason,' Eddie asserted. '[Bonnaroo] makes you realise how it could actually work. And on top of that it's a great fucking night!'

Despite the good vibes at Bonnaroo, not everyone went home happy. Pearl Jam's set overran by around an hour, causing rapper

Kanye West to take the stage at 4.30am instead of 2.45am. West, whose planetary-sized ego was subsequently ridiculed in an April 2009 episode of *South Park*, was less than impressed and put in what can only be described as a below par set. The rapper later apologised that he 'didn't have the ability to give the performance I wanted to', opining, 'sometimes I go two, three days without sleep working on my performance. I have to ice my knees after every show and they hurt when I walk through the airport.'

In August, Eddie took his solo show out for a second, thirteen-date run aimed at taking in the East Coast venues that he had missed the first time around. Despite a subdued reception at the opening gigs in Boston, Vedder hit his stride during the New York leg of the tour on 4 August, playing a 28-song set that incorporated his customary mix of Pearl Jam numbers, cover versions and songs from *Into The Wild*.

The following month saw Jeff release his debut solo album, *Tone*, which was made available via the Ten Club as a limited edition of 3,000 discs. The album was a collection of material that the bassist had written over the past decade that had not been picked up by the band. 'It just got to a point where I had to clean off the shelf a little bit,' he explained. 'I broke this group of 35 songs into three groups and decided to finish one of them.'

Shortly after the release of *Tone*, Stone Gossard announced that his second solo album was almost complete and posted a new track, 'Your Flames', on the band's official site. The new material was a collaboration with singer-songwriter Pete Droge, vocalist Barb Ireland, and multi-instrumentalist Hans Teuber, amongst others, and tied into Timberland's 'Dig It' campaign, an initiative aimed at promoting environmental activism through music. Stone also committed to a string of four dates in support of the Dig It initiative, taking in Boston, New York, Los Angeles and San Francisco during October.

In late 2008, Jeff, Matt, Stone and Mike collaborated on further new Pearl Jam material during a trip to Jeff's Montana home. The bassist revealed that this was 'the first time since the first record that we've really rehearsed . . . instead of just going into the studio with a handful of ideas'. Eddie later added temporary vocals to roughly 50 percent of the material his bandmates had demoed during this period, and in turn submitted his own songs for them to work on, referring to the more intuitive, less self-conscious writing process he embraced at this point as 'like capturing lightning in a bottle'.

'At any moment something fantastic could happen,' Jeff said of the sessions, while Matt Cameron smirked, 'Sometimes you have your best ideas in the bathroom' – a reference to new song 'Johnny Guitar', which was inspired by a Johnny 'Guitar' Watson album cover that Vedder saw pasted above a urinal at the band's rehearsal space.

'You can listen to songs that have meaning,' Vedder said of his newly relaxed approach to his role as songwriter, 'but never know what they mean for decades. It always seemed like the lyrics have to be this, or have to be that, or have to be three-dimensional – but they don't. That's new for me too; participating as an instrument rather than a storyteller. Writing's great, but there are so many words, there's too many options.'

At the start of 2009, Pearl Jam continued to piece together their ninth studio album, *Backspacer*, whilst simultaneously overseeing Brendan O'Brien's remix of *Ten*, which was released in four separate special editions on 24 March 2009. 'The band loved the original mix of *Ten*, but were also interested in what it would sound like if I were to deconstruct and remix it,' explained the producer. 'The original *Ten* sound is what millions of people bought, dug and loved, so I was initially hesitant to mess around with that. After years of persistent nudging from the band, I was able to wrap my head around the idea of offering it as a companion piece to the original – giving a fresh take on it, a more direct sound.'

'I think the fact that we had wanted to take *Ten* and re-mix it, make it sound a little drier,' said Mike McCready, 'and Jeff Ament had wanted this to happen [for] a long time and it finally did. Both of those things [the recording of *Backspacer* and the remixing of *Ten*] kind of coincided at the same time. It probably had some sort of influence on how this new record came out, but I think songwriting-wise I don't believe it did, because I think we're all different people now.'

The remixed, remastered versions of *Ten* represented the first step in a programme of re-issuing enhanced versions of the band's back catalogue ahead of their twentieth anniversary, though by early 2011, only the first three albums had received this treatment.

After a protracted preparation period ('It was all based on this brand-new idea – to us – of "Let's write the songs before we record them,"' smiled Eddie) Pearl Jam finally commenced recording their new album, undertaking a two-week session with O'Brien at Henson Recording Studios in Los Angeles in February 2009 – the first time the band had spent a significant stretch in any studio outside of Seattle since sessions for 1996's *No Code*. '[When] we got together with Ed it really started getting more cohesive,' said Mike, 'we took that momentum down to Los Angeles with Brendan . . . It was a great idea to get out of Seattle. You've gotta get out [of] your comfort zone, and we've talked about doing that for the past ten years and kind of haven't, so we trusted Brendan's judgement.'

The group's trust in O'Brien's judgement extended to allowing the producer to exert more control over the album's sound. 'In the past, Brendan would say, "It's a great song, but I think you should do it in a different key," and we'd say no,' explained Vedder. 'But now that we've heard Bruce [Springsteen] has listened to his suggestions, I think we will too.'

'He [O'Brien] just brings a brutally honest approach to what he thinks is working and what isn't,' said Jeff Ament, 'and it really moves things along . . . We don't get weighed down with ideas that maybe aren't even that good. He's one of the few people outside of the band that we trust with our music.'

Backspacer was eventually completed in April 2009 during a two-week session at Southern Tracks, O'Brien's mixing facility in Atlanta. The album's lyrics – written entirely by Vedder for the first time since *Vitalogy* – exhibited a markedly more positive outlook than that featured on Pearl Jam's previous LPs, with Eddie crediting the election of President Barack Obama as the inspiration behind his newfound lyrical optimism. 'I've tried, over the years, to be hopeful in the lyrics, and I think that's going to be easier now.'

Regarding the album's 'celebratory' vibe, Mike McCready elaborated, 'From my own point of view, I would imagine we've gotten out [from] under eight years of horrible government and we now have a new president and we're all elated and excited about the fact that there's actually some hope and somebody smart in the White House and things are affecting our lives in a way that's positive, where it hadn't been for many, many years. That makes us all US citizens, and in our band, excited about being around right now. I think that has a lot to do with it.'

Lead single 'The Fixer' – a lean, riff-laden power-pop stomper – was written about the male tendency to try and perform easy fixes on broken relationships regardless of what's causing the problem. 'Men, we all think we can fix anything,' explained Vedder. 'It's not necessarily a good thing. In a relationship, a woman will say, "This is wrong," and we're like, "I'll fix that, don't worry about it, we can fix it." These wonderful people, the woman you're in a relationship with, they don't want you to fix it. They just want you to listen to what's happening.'

Focused, optimistic and crammed with gravelly melodies, in its brief 37-minute running time *Backspacer* captured a band at the peak of their powers – older, wiser and as sonically commanding as ever. Album track 'Get Some' was influenced by eighties new-wave pop ('there's a lot of mornings it's hard to get going – this song will do it', claimed Vedder); 'Just Breathe' – triggered by a song Eddie penned for the *Into The Wild* soundtrack and embellished with strings and French horns – was described by Eddie as 'as close to a love song as we've ever gotten'; 'Speed of Sound', a midnight lament from the perspective of a man drinking alone in a bar, stemmed from a songwriting session with Rolling Stones guitarist Ronnie Wood; while 'Force of Nature', a classic slab of grunge, is 'about the strength of one person in the relationship, when they can withstand some of the faults in another'.

Mike McCready summed up *Backspacer* as 'a tight, concise rock'n'roll record with kind of pop or maybe new-wave elements to it', while Vedder declared Pearl Jam's ninth album to be 'stuff we can sink our teeth into'.

'There are a handful of things on this record that I don't know if we've ever really done before,' reflected Jeff Ament. 'Like every good rock band, they should be challenging themselves to kind of get into some new areas. I feel like on this record we have.'

As the band had declined to re-sign their deal with J Records, *Backspacer* was released through Pearl Jam's own label, Monkeywrench Records, in conjunction with Universal Music Group in the US and through Universal's Island Records internationally. During a backstage interview in Berlin when they were touring the album, Matt Cameron explained this decision: 'For us it's been a lot of years signed to record companies, and – although they gave us good support because we signed up in the early days – ultimately you don't own your records, so that's one exciting part of this release: that we do own it, and we're taking control of how it's being released in the States . . . A lot of the decision-making does come from the band, so there's a lot on the table for us, it's definitely a full-time job, even when we're not touring and playing live or making records. There's more work because of it, but ultimately it pays off because we're able to present the group in a real, honest way.'

In August, prior to the album's release, Pearl Jam undertook a ten-date tour of Canada and Europe, previewing their new material in arenas as well as more intimate venues such as London's 2,000-capacity Shepherd's Bush Empire. Sets typically ran to around 30 songs, interspersing covers including Pink Floyd's 'Interstellar Overdrive', Bob Dylan's 'All Along The Watchtower' and the Beatles' 'You've Got To Hide Your Love Away' with previews of the forthcoming album and choice cuts from the band's back catalogue. During the fan-club-only London gig, Vedder called out to members of the audience he recognised and swigged from a bottle of pinot noir. 'Drinking helps a performance,' he told the *Australian* on the day of the gig. 'Absolutely it does. Over the years it's become a sort of tool. I've done shows where I don't drink but they always felt like everyone else was having fun and I was just doing a job.'

Released on 20 September 2009, *Backspacer* went straight in at Number 1 on the *Billboard* Top 200 Chart, with 189,000 copies sold during its first week of release. It was the first of their albums to claim the US top spot since *No Code* thirteen years previously, and also went to Number 1 in Portugal, Croatia, Canada, New Zealand and Australia. It would eventually achieve either gold or platinum status in thirteen different countries. The critical response, like the record-buying public's, was almost unanimously positive. 'This is a record made by mature men with perspective: full of reflection and eclecticism,' wrote the *Guardian*, concluding that 'the Seattle quartet have rarely sounded this energised'. *Rolling Stone* observed that 'after toughing out the Bush years, Pearl Jam aren't in the mood for brooding; at long last, surf's up', while the *Los Angeles Times* declared the album to be 'proof of what a bunch of grown people can accomplish when they know exactly what they want'.

Immediately following the album's release, Pearl Jam performed two shows at Seattle's Key Arena on the 21 and 22 of September, and over the course of the subsequent two months toured the US, Australia and New Zealand (the first time the band had performed in the latter country for over a decade) – their last concert of 2009 was at the AMI Stadium in Christchurch on 29 November, where Eddie led the 30,000-strong crowd in a chorus of 'Happy Birthday' dedicated to Matt Cameron, who had turned 47 the previous day.

Pearl Jam didn't perform live again until May 2010, playing only 26 shows across America and Europe over the course of the second half of the year. 'We give each other space,' explained Mike McCready of the band's stop-start touring cycle, which he credits as integral to their long-term survival. 'That's the biggest reason we're still around,' agreed Jeff Ament. '[There] was a point about '93 or '94 where we sort of disbanded for six months, didn't really talk to one another, didn't really know where each other was at and went off to live life and refuel. It gave us a lot of energy creatively to get away from the bubble.'

On 22 October 2010, it was twenty years to the day since the band first performed together as Mookie Blaylock at Seattle's Off Ramp club. It was perhaps unsurprising that – rather than headlining their own show or indulging in any overblown displays of public self-congratulation – they chose to mark this milestone by once again performing over two nights at Neil Young's annual Bridge School Benefit concert in support of physically impaired children. 'It's perfect for [the anniversary]: not too blown up,' Stone Gossard told *Billboard*. 'It's not about us, it's about all those kids that are onstage with you, and about Neil Young and his commitment, his influence.' These two performances were the last of 2010, and Pearl Jam's collective thoughts inevitably turned towards the follow-up to *Backspacer*. 'The band is definitely going to get together, probably [initially] without Ed and start to hammer out some demos and get some stuff to the point where he can hear it,' confirmed Stone.

In the meantime, fans had *Live On Ten Legs* (an eighteen-track live album recorded over the course of the band's 2003-2010 world tours, released in January 2011) and the twentieth anniversary editions of *Vs.* and *Vitalogy* to occupy themselves with. Announced in February 2011 and released in late March, the Deluxe and Definitive Legacy re-releases of the band's second and third albums included previously unreleased demos, bonus tracks, covers and live recordings.

That same month, Jeff Ament revealed that the band had roughly 25 songs ready for Pearl Jam's tenth studio album and planned to start recording in April. This time, however, the process became dramatically fragmented. 'We started making a record like we normally do,' explained Stone, 'which would be, go into a studio and demo, get a bunch of songs, then go to Los Angeles and record with Brendan O'Brien. Usually in ten or twelve days we can knock out the majority of a record, and we did that [in 2011]. And we got seven or eight songs done, and I think, in retrospect, we looked back and went, "Okay, we've got five, really. They're cool." And then we realised we have half a record, then time slipped away. And *PJ Twenty* came out, and there was this other stuff happening.'

Directed by *Rolling Stone* journalist-turned-filmmaker Cameron Crowe (known for movies including *Singles* and *Almost Famous*) and released to coincide with the band's twentieth anniversary, the *Pearl Jam Twenty* documentary took a candid look back at the highs and lows of the group's two decades together. Crowe, a fan and longtime friend of the band since their early days in Seattle, had a team of researchers sift through approximately 30,000 hours of video footage in order to assemble the warm-hearted, two-hour retrospective.

The promotional campaign surrounding the film's release in September 2011, combined with preparation for their twentieth anniversary tour, proved sufficiently distracting for the band to temporarily abandon work on the new album. *Pearl Jam Twenty* grossed nearly half a million dollars at the US box office.

The Pearl Jam Twenty, or PJ20, tour got underway in East Troy, Wisconsin, with a two-day festival held over the Labour Day Weekend. Attended by tens of thousands, the festival included a museum where fans could view band artifacts. '[People said] this ain't gonna happen,' Vedder told the audience of the band reaching their twentieth year together. 'That it's a dream, against the odds. I'm glad we didn't listen.' They were joined onstage by the Strokes' Julian Casablancas (who provided vocals on 'Not For You'), Josh Homme of Queens of the Stone Age, and Chris Cornell (who duetted with Vedder on a powerful rendition of 'Hunger Strike'). The tour subsequently moved through North and Latin America, concluding in Mexico City on 24 November 2011.

'I'm surprised that we're around still,' said Mike McCready. 'A lot of the bands that we . . . came out with are not around. We've been around for 21, 22 years. I don't know what it is. It's not being around each other a bunch, then being around each other a bunch. Getting away from each other. But also having humour and the same kind of silly inside jokes that we've always had.'

The self-proclaimed 'ultimate dad band' wouldn't head out on the road again until June 2012, focusing on their families during this hiatus. Eddie, father to two young daughters, Harper and Olivia, joked: 'I can only practice once a week, after eight o'clock, after the kids are in bed; maybe Thursdays after the carpool.'

They eventually headed back into the studio in 2013 to complete work on the follow-up to *Backspacer*. '[In total] it was kind of two ten-day sessions in Los Angeles, and then maybe a three-week mixing, finishing session,' Stone explained during an interview with Sleater-Kinney's Carrie Brownstein. 'So it wasn't that much time, in terms of the actual time working on the record, but it seems normal and natural that we're not cranking records out every year and a half. It feels like a good thing that we're not in a rush to get something out. I don't know if we would've had the patience for that, earlier on, I think we would've just forced it out. It's good that we're not racing.'

The product of these sessions was the twelve-track album, *Lightning Bolt*. Largely devoid of *Backspacer*'s pop sensibilities and brevity, it was welcomed by fans and critics as a return to form. Treading a fine line between pile-driving rock stompers designed to shake arenas and more contemplative moments, such as Pink Floyd indebted piano ballad 'Sirens', the album reflected the duality of its recording process, with the divide between the 2011 and 2013 studio sessions evident in the softer and harder songs. 'The first batch of songs we did was more mid-tempo,' said Stone, 'and sounded a little bit slick. And we knew that with the next batch we really wanted to get some energy going and get some rock songs going. The up-tempo stuff is all from the last session.'

The first sessions are well represented by the twanging guitars and mournful lyricism of 'Sleeping By Myself', and tender acoustic balladry of country-inflected album closer 'Future Days'. While the adrenaline-charged title track's air-punching harmonies, and the cathartic chorus and buzz-saw guitars that anchor ode to nature 'Swallowed Whole', tell the other side of the story. Age and fatherhood may have mellowed Pearl Jam, but you'd be hard pushed to hear the evidence.

Preceded by lead single, 'Mind Your Manners' (a mosh-pit-friendly number reminiscent of a leaner, less alcohol-muddied Motörhead) and finally released on 15 October 2013 – more than four years after *Backspacer* – *Lightning Bolt* once again demonstrated the unwavering devotion of the band's fan base, reaching Number 1 on the US, Canadian and Australian album charts. It was the fifth album of their career to hit the top spot on the *Billboard* 200 chart, with first-week sales of 166,000 copies.

'I mean, it's kind of like dying, or getting older,' said Eddie of the group's longevity. 'You don't want to get older, but what are the options? And so for us, in a way, it's like, what are the options, to not be in a group? It's like you wanna just keep living and still be in a band. It's life or death.'

'For me it's always been chemistry,' said Matt Cameron, 'the way people come together to form a band or join or a band . . . To get that really unique chemistry that allows you to continue to write music and continue to grow as a group. It's kind of rare, especially in our case, we've been doing it for so long. We definitely hit good peaks and valleys, to this day, I think. It still feels good to do it, as a creative entity. And songs. You gotta have songs.'

And songs they had. For *Rolling Stone*, the album cemented Pearl Jam's status as 'America's foremost torchbearers of classic rock'. The *New York Times*' verdict was equally positive: '[PJ are] grown-ups with fewer demons and more polish, but they're still pushing themselves.' As for the Vedder, he'd lost none of his ability to 'angst', agonising over the huge universal themes of 'mortality and faith'. *Kerrang!* offered the highest praise, concluding: 'It's fast, it's slow, it's mature without being boring; it rocks, even when it doesn't. It's also one of the best albums of 2013, if not the best.'

On 11 October, the band embarked on a North American tour. Tipped by *Rolling Stone* as one of the hottest tickets of 2013, it ran from coast to coast, via Canada, before finally winding up with an epic three-and-a-half-hour homecoming show at Seattle's Key Arena on 6 December. 'We don't have to travel anywhere, so we can give it all we got,' Eddie quipped. Somewhere amid two extended encores, Pearl Jam were joined by Soundgarden guitarist Kim Thayil and Mudhoney's Mark Arm and Steve Turner for a raucous, climactic cover of MC5's 'Kick Out The Jams'.

Pearl Jam saw in 2014 with a headlining slot at Australia's Big Day Out Festival in January. Topping a bill which included Snoop Dogg and Mudhoney, Pearl Jam put on a memorable performance. The highlight of the show was an impromptu duet with Arcade Fire frontman Win Butler, who joined the band onstage for a cover of Neil Young's anthem, 'Rockin' in the Free World'. Post-festival, Pearl Jam disbanded to pursue their individual commitments, with the exception of Eddie. Armed with his beloved ukulele, Vedder seized the opportunity to undertake a solo tour Down Under. These stripped-back sets offered an entirely different experience from the Lightning Bolt tour, which reconvened in Amsterdam on 16 June. One of the string of European dates that followed was held at the 65,000-capacity Milton Keynes Bowl in the UK on 11 July.

Despite the rapturous welcome Pearl Jam received that day – it was their thirtieth and biggest ever gig on UK soil, with guest appearances from Pete Townshend's brother and George Harrison's son amongst other rock royalty – some of those in attendance were less than impressed by Eddie's politicised performance. Earnest to a fault, the frontman set about reaffirming his deep-seated pacifist convictions live onstage. 'I swear to God, there are some people out there who are looking for a reason to kill,' he told the crowd, mid-way through a blistering rendition of 'Daughter'. 'They're looking for a reason to go across borders and take over land that doesn't belong to them. They should get the fuck out and mind their own fucking business.' Given the simmering tension in the Middle East, certain pro-Israeli fans leapt on Eddie's impassioned monologue as a thinly veiled jibe at their people. Israeli rock DJ Ben Red fired back with an accusatory open letter, warning Vedder to stay away from Israel now that his 'true face has finally been revealed'. Eddie's response was characteristically heartfelt. Whilst unwilling to retract his comments – after all, he'd made no direct reference to Israel – he made every effort to explain his emotional response to the conflict. 'War hurts no matter which sides the bombs are falling on,' he wrote in a statement of his own. 'With about a dozen assorted ongoing conflicts in the news every day . . . some of us feel the need to reach out to others to see if we are not alone in our outrage. That's not something I'm going to stop any time soon. I'd rather be naïve, heartfelt and hopeful than resigned to say nothing for fear of misinterpretation and retribution.'

Driven by the same powerful conviction, Pearl Jam have remained as dedicated a crew of activists as ever. Since completing the final leg of the Lightning Bolt tour in October 2014, PJ have occupied themselves with philanthropic projects great and small, from re-homing Toni Wood (mother of tragic Mother Love Bone frontman Andrew Wood) to orchestrating a once-in-a-lifetime charity gig with Pete Townshend. The proceeds from this star-studded benefit, held at Chicago's Rosemont Theatre in May 2015, went to Teen Cancer America. In July, Pearl Jam were unveiled as headliners of the Global Citizen Festival. Scheduled for 26 September in New York's historic Central Park, tickets for this event can be won by 'engaging' with your cause of choice online. 'We hope fans will sign up,' explained Stone, 'not just to earn tickets to the show, but to be part of a movement.'

Fortunately, these extra-curricular commitments are not to keep Pearl Jam off the road. To the delight of their Latin American fans, the band will play Chile, Argentina, Brazil, Columbia and Mexico in November 2015. Despite the accolades currently being heaped upon his band (in February 2015, Pearl Jam scooped their second Grammy Award, winning 'Best Recording Package' for *Lightning Bolt*), Vedder takes no part of success for granted. 'My type of personality is that even when things are going really good, then I just feel like something bad could happen at any minute,' he reflected. 'It's like surfing, especially if you're on a big wave, as soon as you think you've got it, and don't pay attention for a second, then a wipe-out will soon follow. I think a lot about the fragility of life. I just feel it at all times.'

Yet, for all his misgivings, Eddie Vedder remains the nucleus of Pearl Jam. His public persona, and his personal mood swings, have seen him switch from idealistic zeal to cynical indifference; from reluctant underground icon to arrogant rock god; from an almost zen-like self-control to frayed mental anguish.

What remains consistent is that Eddie Vedder and Pearl Jam stay true to their own sense of personal integrity. Whether howling from the moral high ground or speaking from the ground-level perspective of an everyman, Eddie remains all too human. 'It's not hard to be a rock star,' he's said in the past. 'If you want to go around fucking women and cleaning a bunch of teenagers of all their dough because they like your band and charge them up the ying for t-shirts and concert tickets, that's easy.'

Instead, more than two decades on from Pearl Jam's first major success, Eddie Vedder flits between adulation and anonymity – a device that maintains his sanity. 'I've got a '64 Plymouth outside,' he told *Kerrang!* during interviews for *Riot Act*. 'I've had it for ten years, it's a little beat up . . . I'm going to put the top down on this rare sunny Seattle day, I'm going to drive home and nobody's going to recognise me . . . I can stop at a light, I can have ten fifteen-year-olds walking in front of the car and I look like an old man behind the wheel of an old car.'

Though the music matters as deadly seriously as ever, his philosophical new outlook lets him survive within a world that can drive sensitive types, like the tragic Kurt Cobain, to their destruction.

'Back in the day,' recalls Eddie, 'I would drive the same road and I'd have people putting themselves in danger trying to shout at me from alongside me. I'm thinking, "Well, you're gonna die by rear-ending the back of that truck if you're not careful." Those panic-type situations, I don't miss them at all,' he reflects, as grounded a human being as any modern rock star could ever hope to be.

'Roger Daltrey has this thing he always says: "Be lucky,"' explained Ed. 'It took me a few years to reach it, but I took his advice.' In an interview with *Rolling Stone*, Ament hinted at the prospect of an eleventh studio album. 'Everybody's got some stuffed stowed away,' was his tantalising reveal. Here's hoping that Pearl Jam – and their fans – will stay lucky for many years to come.